JOURNEY THROUGH GRIEF

ROBERT A. WILLIAMS

THOMAS NELSON PUBLISHERS
Nashville

Published in Nashville, Tennessee, by Thomas
Nelson, Inc., and distributed in Canada by Lawson
Falle, Ltd., Cambridge, Ontario.

Scripture quotations are from the NEW KING
JAMES VERSION of the Bible. Copyright ©
1979, 1980, 1982, Thomas Nelson, Inc.,
Publishers.

**Library of Congress
Cataloging-in-Publication Data**

Williams, Robert A., 1939–
        Journey through grief / Robert A. Williams.
            p.   cm.
        Includes bibliographical references.
        ISBN 0-8407-3165-5
        1. Consolation.   2. Bereavement—Religious
aspects—Christianity.
        3. Williams, Robert A., 1939–   I. Title.
BV4905.2.W5351991a   90-49902
                                                            CIP

Printed in the United States of America

1 2 3 4 5 6 7 — 96 95 94 93 92 91

CONTENTS

————o————

In Memory of
Those Persons Mentioned in the
Introduction of This Volume
and
in Honor of
Their Families and Friends

ACKNOWLEDGMENTS

———o———

Journey Through Grief was prompted by my own struggle over a series of deaths among my family and intimate friends, each of which occurred in the space of one year. Were it not for the pain experienced and the warm memories challenging me, the writing of the book would never have been entertained. I give tribute to those among my family: to my brother, Ron Williams; to my brother-in-law, Joe Roberts; to my sister-in-law, Alice Segovis. Tribute must go also to those among my friends: to my best friend, Creath Davis; to my other intimate friends, John Allison, George Clark, Roy Downey and Hugo Schoellkopf.

I am especially indebted to those whose recent losses were an ever-present incentive for me to complete the writing. Among these are the families of Sybil Allison, Ann Clark, Verdell Davis, Lindy Downey, Lucy Mabery, Alma Roberts, Gail Schoellkopf, Bob Segovis, and Judy Williams.

As always, many friends served as helpful

reader-consultants and affirming partners in the progression of the book. Among these are Jim and Frances Almond, Jim and Allene Hemingway, James and Pat Gibson, Don and Karen Kreager, M.B. and Netty Nelson, Glen and Dot Reddell, Bill and Peggy Simpkin, and Donna Tupman Walker.

I credit the making of the book to those under the publishing auspices of Thomas Nelson Press: to Ron Haynes, Senior Acquisitions Editor, who first reviewed the manuscript and moved it through its various stages; to Cynthia Tripp, Copy Editor, whose amending of the typescript helped superbly in the unity and coherence of the book; and to Jennifer Farrar and Susan Salmon, Editors, who helped with the final production phases of the book.

The following persons graciously consented to read the galleys: Dr. John Claypool, my former pastor and author of *Tracks of A Fellow Struggler;* Dr. John P. Newport, my major professor at Southwestern Baptist Theological Seminary; Dr. James Pleitz, Senior Minister of Park Cities Baptist Church, Dallas, Texas, my current pastor; and a long-time friend, Dr. Kenneth Wiggins, a child psychiatrist in the Dallas metropolitan area.

Finally, the work would have been poorly pieced together without the stenographic expertise of my wife, Eve, who typed and retyped the manuscript through every phase of production. Much credit goes to her, also, in her standing as a bulwark of strength while suffering the same grief that prompted my own expression in these pages.

PREFACE

———◦———

One hardly needs a preface to the subject of this book, as everyone has experienced grief to some degree and will more than likely experience it again and again along life's journey.

I am not writing another book on grief because there are too few on the subject already in print, but because the proverbial last word on grief has not yet been written. Nor will it be as long as there are bereaved persons in the world. There are always new experiences and new meanings that must be addressed, ones that former books do not cover. I hope this book will speak to some of your individual needs now and in the future.

Every person's confrontation with sorrow is uniquely his or her own. Some books may speak to that unique sorrow, while others are unconsoling altogether. *Journey Through Grief* is no different, in this sense. Some readers may profit more than others. Try to read the book, then, as you might winnow wheat—keep the kernels and blow away the chaff.

I present *Journey Through Grief* not as a cure-all for the bereaved, but as one more attempt by a fellow traveler to understand the struggle of the ones left behind. If I seem to have missed the mark in your case, I offer my sincere apology. At the same time, I hope that you find the source that will be effective in your own emotional recovery.

I have written out of my own struggles and with the awareness of the more crucial struggles of those to whom this book is dedicated and for whom it has largely been written. My impetus is that of obedience to God, who impelled me into the effort as a gift to those who sorrow.

If I can help to "satisfy the desire of the afflicted," or help to "raise up the foundations" that have been destroyed by grief, or in a measure be a "repairer of the breach" that has been caused by death, then the effort in writing this book will far and away suffice as its own reward (Isa. 58:10–12). One needs no pay, no prize, no honor, where healing of sorrow rises.

INTRODUCTION: "STILLE NACHT"

---○---

When she had passed, it seemed like the ceasing of exquisite music.

Henry Wadsworth Longfellow, *Evangeline*

He lives, he wakes—'tis Death is dead, not he.

Percy Bysshe Shelley, *Adonais* XLI

The moment I arrived home I knew something was wrong. My wife, Eve, always an inspiring presence, sat rather dolefully on the sofa. Then came the reason for the somber mood so uncharacteristic of her: Her sister, Alma, in Virginia had just called with the shocking news that her husband, Joe, had died of a heart attack. A phenomenon so final as death happening to Joe, always a healthy man, seemed so impossible. Only a few months earlier, he was visibly hearty as he joked with us and led us on a tour of his home workshop where we viewed a number of fascinating pieces of furniture that he had made for himself and other family members. This eventful day of the call started out no differently. Joe had just come from the workshop to eat with the family, when a sudden weakness came over him. He thought that if he would lie down, the weakness would pass momentarily. Lying on his bed, he was suddenly gripped with chest pains. In a matter of minutes, he was dead. Alma, disbelieving and almost in a state of denial, was understandably devastated. Eve and I set off for Virginia the following day to face death with her and the family.

Not many months later, Eve's brother-in-law, Bob, called. He said that Eve's sister, Alice, was in the hospital in Conroe, Texas, and was not expected to live. We were equally staggered by this news as with Joe's death but for a different reason. We were aware that Alice had cancer of the bone marrow, but with every telephone conversation she had played down the severity of her illness. She was a tough and driven personality, not given to moaning her condition. She would tell us that according to her doctors this type of cancer could take years to develop. She would tell us she was in a state of remission and doing fine. Understandably, the call that she was on the verge of death was unbelieveable to us.

We spent the next two and a half weeks away from home, practically living at the hospital, hoping against hope for Alice's recovery. It never came. Alice breathed her last before our eyes as we stood watch with her husband and children. Again, we were beaten by death.

But death was only a temporary transition. For a while, during the last hour, the labored breathing and involuntary moans of her dying drove our hearts into our throats. Heavy sedation saved her from so much conscious pain, and we were grateful. But in a single moment, without any warning, her breathing stopped. Death had done its work; the pain was over. Life, a different kind of life, took up where death left off. The sensation suddenly struck me that I was looking at the greatest evidence of peace I had ever seen. This peace seemed to whisper that death itself had died. Alice's body was still. She could feel no more agony. Our loss was great, but the silence was God's way of turning up the volume on life. I knew the reality of the psalmist's words, "Be still, and know that I am God" (Ps. 46:10).

As I reflected upon Alice's peace, I recalled a time only a few years earlier when Eve and I experienced a similar silence. We were sleeping in a hotel in Jerusalem, when, about four o'clock in the morning, I woke up. The sensation of stillness all around seemed incredibly strange. There were no detectable sounds anywhere. There were no cars moving outside, no voices in the hallway, no crickets chirping, not even the stirring of animals in the street below. I lay there for ten minutes listening to the silence, until it was broken faintly by a dog barking in the distance. I got out of bed, raising the window carefully so as not to disturb the quietness. I sat there on the floor, peering into the predawn sky still brilliant with starlight. After a few moments alone, I awakened Eve and whispered to her to join me. We sat together, listening to the silence. That was one of my first intimate encounters with peace.

Sitting in Jerusalem, my thoughts drifted to the nearby village of Bethlehem. Phillips Brooks' familiar Christmas carol came to mind:

> O little town of Bethlehem,
>   How still we see thee lie!
> Above thy deep and dreamless sleep
>   The silent stars go by;
> Yet in thy dark streets shineth
>   The Everlasting Light.
> The hopes and fears of all the years
>   Are met in thee tonight.

Close behind that quiet reminder of God's greatest Peace came the words of *Stille Nacht (Silent Night)* by German composer Joseph Mohr:

Silent night, holy night
　All is calm, all is bright
'Round yon Virgin Mother and Child.
　Holy Infant so tender and mild,
Sleep in heavenly peace,
　Sleep in heavenly peace.

That stillness, that silence, that peace is what I felt again the moment Alice took her last breath. We left the room and went to the hospital chapel where, in our own way, we bade her "sleep in heavenly peace."

Praying in the chapel, I thought of an evening when Eve and I had sat at Alice's bedside. Perhaps Eve had dozed off from exhaustion or maybe she was reading to escape a little while the intensity of her sister's suffering. In any case, I slipped over to the bed, touched Alice's hand, and sent up a silent prayer. Or it may have been a plea. I prayed something to the effect of: "Lord, this woman loves You deeply. Couldn't You take her into consideration, raise her from this sickbed and to life; restore her to the love of her husband and family; and give her the reprieve of Your grace?"

I heard no voices, received no instant computer printout of answers, but I seemed to sense how God would answer my question. It came quickly. He gave it to me straight—at least

15

to my way of thinking: "Yes, I could raise her, but then I would have to be consistent. I would have to consider every other person suffering in this world too.

"I would also have to interrupt the natural laws that I set into motion. Yes, I know that nature groans and travails against the moral collapse of the world as you know it. I know, too, that the result of sin is death and that I have mastered both in my Son. But if I intervened in this world of natural law and moral consequence every time a brick fell from a building as a God-fearing person was walking below, would I not have to do it for the nonbeliever as well? And if so, wouldn't I be creating a stranger and more unjust world than we already have?

"No. I may seem to lose a few skirmishes to disease or 'accidents,' but I will win the war with sin and death for the life of the world. My Son has already defeated both. The victory will be ours. This whole grieving world awaits the redemption of my people. I'm laboring, through Jesus, to heal the rift in the universe, both physical and spiritual. Please believe me! Please bear with me. Please accept what I choose as best for everyone—even you, my son; even you, my daughter. Please believe, won't you?"

Our only possible response, as thought-worn,

weary pilgrims of our God, is: "Lord, I believe. Help thou my unbelief!"

Other members of our family have also died this year. My brother-in-law lost his father, and only recently a brother. I have lost two aunts within two months of each other.

After all this, we hoped that this difficult year would progress into a more benevolent one. It wasn't to be. On December 7, we received another call that my brother, Ron, had died that morning of a massive heart attack. As a petroleum engineer, he was working offshore on a drilling rig, talking with a friend in the log room, when he suddenly fainted, giving no preliminary inkling of a problem. Within minutes a helicopter carried him to a nearby hospital in Morgan City, Louisiana, where he was pronounced dead on arrival.

The funeral was unbelievably sad for all of us. For me, the difficult time had come. My nephew, a freshman in high school, requested that I bring the message at his father's memorial service. I thank God for the confidence and assurance that He gave for that assignment. Such is not the least nor the last of life's tough assignments. Other similar appointments await us down the road, but none will prove so demanding that the strength of our Lord will not be adequate. We will learn soon enough that Christ and Christianity are for the tough-minded, but that only the courageous Christ in our lives makes it possible for any of us to survive the burden at all.

In April, long-time friend John Allison died untimely of a heart attack while sitting at his desk. We had shared in Christian fellowship groups over the years and had enjoyed the camaraderie of seasonal wild game hunts many times. He had been our intimate friend and an encouragement to many others in our circle.

Two months after John's death, almost to the day, three other friends of ours, along with a fourth man we had not known, were killed in a plane crash in the mountains of Wyoming. Among these was my best friend of twenty-eight years, Creath Davis. No other loss has ever affected me as deeply. Here was a brother, a confidante, a spiritual partner who had more input into my life as a friend than possibly anyone else I have known. His wife, Verdell, and the children they reared so nobly, have left lasting family marks upon us throughout the years.

Much also could be said of two other friends in the crash, Hugo Schoellkopf and George Clark, who in every way showed themselves to be God's men—in the way they loved their families, in the way they ran their businesses, in the manner in which they related to people as a whole. Their families continue to bless everyone around them.

Three months later, another friend, Roy Downey, died after a two-year bout with cancer. All during his illness we prayed on a daily basis. We called and wrote to friends, asking them to pray for him and his wife, Lindy, his daughter, Laurie, and his son, Drew. We tried to encourage God to see it our way. One day Lindy received a copy of a letter we had written to more than one hundred of our friends, asking for their prayers on Roy's behalf. She promptly took the letter upstairs and, showing it to Roy, half-jokingly said, "I know that God is going to heal you, because Robert is not going to leave him alone until he does!" I wish persistence were, indeed, the answer, for persistent I was. But God has greater wisdom in matters too deep and mysterious for the human mind to understand. But if in a small measure, we were able to help a man die well, that is satisfaction enough for now. The total answer will come when we meet again.

Just a few weeks before Roy's death, a loss came that bordered on the experience of death itself. We were near completion of an upstairs remodeling of the home of Lloyd and Dee Jones. The work crew had just lacquered the wanescote of a bedroom and were closing the windows to go home. Suddenly, when one of the men moved a fan from an open window in the room, the cord sparked in the electrical outlet and set off a flash fire that instantly swept the room, ultimately damaging most of the upstairs. Dee, though visibly shaken, took the ordeal in stride because of her deep values and sensitivity as a Christian. Only after the fire was out and we stood at the foot of the stairwell looking up into the burned-out corridor, Dee began to cry. I tried to comfort her by assuring her that we would rebuild the house better than the original. "I know," she said, still crying, "but it is like watching someone die!" The truth of that statement struck a chord with us more than she knew, but we have begun the rebuilding process of "resurrecting" that dead entity into a thing of beauty.

Without spiritualizing a valid fact of the Christian faith, I think that is very close to what Jesus is now doing for these, our friends, whom we have temporarily lost. He bears with us, whom they left behind, the burden of grief. He walks through the valley of the shadow of death holding our hand. He encourages us to keep walking. He helps us to grieve well. I can envision God saying to each of us, "I know how you feel. It hurts me too. I can sympathize with you; I had to watch my Son die. But through him, I will resurrect this one whom you loved into a thing of astounding beauty and symmetry, and I'll bring you together again. Trust me, if you can!"

All this is to say that the past year has been—for my wife and me and our community of believers—a harrowing one. I say this not begrudgingly, but soberly. Despite its turbulence, God has used this time in mighty ways. If I did not know that God draws meaning out of every event, I would have every reason to despair. Healing has come slowly, and often only in small patches. We are not through the healing yet, by any means, but enough has come for us to see the progress of hope.

Because we are healing, light is dawning, and our characters are being strengthened. I think I am more excited about life now than in any other season of my journey with the Lord. He is moving me in directions that I may never have considered otherwise. That is why, although I could begrudge the losses, I do so cautiously because I have a vital faith in the total sovereignty of God and in the adequacy of his Son, Jesus Christ.

In retrospect, when one faces so much death in such a short time, one really sees how utterly helpless is man, left to himself. Death is the greatest proof that humanism as a philosophy of

21

life is fruitless! Man cannot make it on his own. Let him approach death pulling himself up by his own bootstraps, and he will see how fatal is his attempt.

How many times in recent months have I heard from my Christian friends the solicitous question: "How do people cope with the death of a loved one without the knowledge and support of a loving God?" I am just as amazed as they that anyone would try. Christianity may not have all the answers to the mysteries of life and death, but she has the Royal Answer in the Person of Jesus Christ, whose real presence stands sentry over the human heart that believes. There is no greater source of support for one's journey through grief, than he who knows all about it because he has, himself, been victorious over it. So, too, will our journey end in victory!

1

Grief as a Journey

Grief is like a journey one must take on a winding mountainside, often seeing the same scenery many times, a road which eventually leads to somewhere we've never been before.
—Gladys M. Hunt[1]

God built a lot of rebound into human beings. The buoyancy of man can be attributed partially to the preciousness of life offered by God as a gift to him and partially to the meaning that somehow resides in every human breast.

As I think of these two aspects that so many times have kept us afloat when we might otherwise have given up, I recall a grueling ordeal that transpired in Midland, Texas. Eighteen-month-old Jessica McClure had fallen into an abandoned water well and was stuck there for three days while workers worked around the clock drilling additional shafts to the point in the casing where they calculated that she might be freed. Besides the many workmen who fought indefatigably to reach the child, hundreds of citizens and friends of the family stood by tirelessly in support of the family. The event drew national attention, as the human heartbeat went out to one tiny life because that life was considered to be more precious than any other major concern of the day.

A SPIRIT OF REBOUND

The superhuman feat of rescuing that child rested in the buoyancy of man to face and deal with the impossible. A central figure in the struggle was a workman who shipped his tools and equipment to the location and labored unstintingly throughout the ordeal, until that happy moment when the bundled pride and joy of those parents emerged from the shaft strapped to a specially devised body splint and drawn to the surface by a cable. At that very moment shouts of joy and applause arose even from those watching on television in their homes. And there were tears amid the laughter. This one worker who had invested so much in the recovery was later interviewed by a television newsperson. His most gripping comment was: "The rock was the hardest I've ever seen, but it was no match for the human spirit."

Almighty God built into the alchemy of the human race an undespairing spirit of rebound. If the preciousness of life and its meaning is present, there is no measuring the ability of man to respond with all there is in him. There is no challenge too great, no danger too fearful! Resiliency, without a doubt, is one of God's great gifts to man.

The need for this resiliency, this rebound, is never more greatly felt than in times of suffering and grief. True, grief has many faces, from initial shock to anger and protest; from numbness to emptiness and disorganization; from pining and yearning to pain and tension; from weeping and loneliness to panic and fearfulness. Look sharply at what has been surrendered in the loss, and little wonder that the tension cuts so deeply. Everything at first appears fatalistic, vacuous, hopeless. Though dismal, however, all of these feelings reach out for some faint hope. Only with the productive facing of our losses and hurts, deeply felt, is there hope in the journey through grief.

I use these three words advisedly because grief is a journey. Resiliency or the lack of it shortens or lengthens that journey. Grief backtracks all the cherished roads previously taken with those we loved, whom now we have protestingly given up in death. Amassing all the memorable events that gave meaning to our lives has taken immeasurable time. Therefore, it takes time, courage, and grace retracking that memorable context and coming to grips with the feelings that it elicits. That journey is almost like the surgical removal of some part of our body. Such is a painful incision into what has been precious to us, and even more painful when we realize that it has been taken from us for the remainder of our earthly lives.

The length of grief's journey is unique to each individual, even as the context of past life together is distinct from that of others. The healing of emotional stress with regard to time is not unlike the healing of the body. Several people may cut their hands and each may experience a different length of time in the healing process. One may heal within a week, another in ten days, and another in three weeks or perhaps longer. The same is true with the wound of grief. We may start the journey of grief together, experiencing some of the same emotional symptoms, but we may or may not reach the completed destination at the same time. This does not mean that we cannot make the emotional journey together and support one another on the way; it simply means that we may not recover at the same pace or experience all the same effects along the way.

ENDURING THE JOURNEY

What seems to be clear about grief as a journey is that it always registers as a bad dream, a nightmare. The experiencing of pain in grief, unfortunately, is the only means of resolving it. William Cowper wrote: "Grief is itself a medicine." Feelings are only healed by being experienced and expressed on a daily basis. Though grief is a daily trial of saying "good-bye" in many ways, the experiencing of the pain is itself the only remedy; to bottle up the agony is to compress it only momentarily. One day the bottle will break and make a terrible mess; and if it does not break, the pain and misery only multiply and build up pressure to an explosive pitch.

Unexpressed grief indicates that the individual has either refused to accept his grief or has lost the will to face his natural feelings of anguish. Alexander McLaren once wrote: "A grief accepted loses most of its power to sadden, and all its power to perturb. It is not outward calamities, but a rebellious will that troubles us." The responsible facing of grief indicates, on the other hand, the responsible will to heal. And healing will come as one bears strength to see the journey through.

Enduring the journey does not mean escaping the normal responsibilities of life. Obviously, having to handle the normal daily responsibilities makes the healing of the wound difficult, as well as different for each grieving person. Some experience the loss of a breadwinner and face the necessity of a work schedule in order to sustain life. Others are left with the responsibility of rearing small children alone. Others find themselves facing life alone, having to seek new ways of filling their time responsibly. No matter what the responsibilities, each deals with a daily flood of loneliness.

We learn to meet our responsibilities with the reality of grief in the foreground. We must realize, too, that responsibilities pressed upon us may actually be a boon to our healing process. There is nothing so destructive as having time on our hands, waiting simply for time to alleviate our pain. Though the resolution of grief is a healing process, the simple passing of time in itself is not. Filling the vacuum with responsibilities is not necessarily an escape from dealing with our grief so much as it helps us to realize our need to experience the grief in the course of our lives and not apart from it.

New days bring new emotions to face just as the progress of any journey brings new scenery before us that we have not previously encountered. We must be ready at any moment to chance upon some symbol of our grief that reminds us of the person whom we lost. Some symbols, of course, recall cherished memories which we do not want or need to remove. Sooner or later those symbols will raise feelings of pride and joy without the attending painfulness. In the interim, however, we should be prepared at all times to face such emotions as are certain to come when we uncover some symbol of our loss—a gift, a letter, a forgotten snapshot, anything that revives feelings of past cherished experiences.

There is no way to guard against reliving those experiences. The only way to *reclaim* the rich value of those times together is actually to *relive* them momentarily—and then to *release* them to God as part of that life which we have already released to Him. Once that segment of past experience is safe with God, we free ourselves from having to cling to it any longer. One day it will fall into that indescribable realm of painless joy. Thus the order of recovery is 1) relive, 2) release, and 3) reclaim.

PURPOSE AND COMPLETION

Little by little we work through a lifetime of reminders until one day the old buoyancy returns and we move into life with a new sense of excitement. Actually, the purpose of grief as a journey is to help us recover our capacity for life, to give us time to regain a renewed vision of purpose, meaning, and excitement about life. That we experience a lot of pain in the process does not detract from our need to complete our grief for the re-investment of our lives.

All journeys end. Grief, too, will be completed. We must sooner or later convince ourselves that our love for the deceased is not in any way proven by the time endurance of our grief. The intensity of our sorrow can cease without our denying our love and honor of the one we cherished. The final turning loose comes at its own pace, but it must inevitably come. If it does not, the grief will turn into clinical depression. Then, rather than reinstating life, we will be enthroning sickness. If we thought grief was painful, we need only experience the devastation of depression which comes through unresolved grief. Giving up on life, which indicates the most serious form of depression, actually ends in our own submissive death.

These kinds of severe feelings are natural, even expected in the early stages of grief (how often we have heard the grief-stricken state that they no longer have anything to live for), but such feelings at long last must be replaced with feelings of resolve and recovery. The journey through grief must come to its appropriate end. We know that it is possible, because God built such rebound into every life—even yours!

Completing grief, however, is the most difficult of all. It not only clings to us, but we feel the need to cling to it, as it seems to be the only thing left of the past. The object of our grief seems ever with us.

In the midst of grief, the boundary between yesterday and today is thin indeed. Six months, even a year later, seems forever like yesterday. How difficult to think there will ever be another tomorrow, when we have such trouble getting yesterday past today.

Because yesterdays haunt us emotionally, we have difficulty seeing what use the future holds for us. Seemingly, our future died with the death of the one we cherished. At this point we cannot really live without the obsessive memories or walking without one foot in the past. If the past relationship had been miserable, hurtful, or disruptive in any sense, the loss would not disable us so emotionally. But if the relationship meant everything to us, then nothing seems adequate at the moment to take its place. As my university teacher used to say, "Once you have tasted the deep red burgundy of life, you don't want to go back to eating sawdust."

The deeper the love and unity in a relationship, the longer it takes to work through the pain of having had to give it up. But the healing will be deeper and more far-reaching due to the depth experienced. The past accomplishment of that depth is the mature foundation from which a power and greatness can be drawn for our return to life. Better to suffer through the depths of unity lost than to suffer through fragments of a relationship that knew not unity or love.

GRIEF'S SLOW STAIN

Grief changes us. Even when we are not conscious of the changes being made, grief's slow stain begins and continues to color our lives along the journey. The change is largely imperceptible until one day we awaken and realize that we are no longer the same. We are different, eternally different, for better or for worse.

The process of change in the effort toward recovery is grindingly slow; and it is slow precisely because of the deep-seated emotions that we are being asked to give up, but which we do not want to give up. In the early stages of grief, *attachment* overshadows *attitude*. As a result, the whole spectrum of life slows down because our natural tendency is to "hold on." We are faced with what Lord Passfield (Sidney Webb) called "the inevitability of gradualness," and what Edmund Burke described as "the silent touches of time." Life, for the moment, is short-circuited; its flow is diverted, its focus narrowed.

In this slowing of life, especially for those who have lost a spouse, days seem never to end and nights seem even longer. Time loses all significance to us except for the fact that it must be endured, and invariably it is endured without any substantial desire flowing from the center of our lives. We detest the clock on the wall because it cannot turn back and it will not speed up. We are left to ride out our inner storm with our emotional system out of "sync" with time.

Harmony is not naturally part of the human condition, but it can be made to be so. Grief, if anything, enhances the disunity. This off-beat sensation, in fact, is what we experience when faced with the torment of grief. We are out of sync with time and the rhythm of life going on around us. Our tempo is out of cadence with the flutter and stir of both the personal state of affairs and the tide of events. But we can change our tempo. We may be grateful that, as living beings, we are not bound to the disharmony. Under God we can pick up the beat and fall into unison again with those we love and with the life we cherish.

Our coming to that crucial point of ascendancy does not mean that we will avoid anguish, depression, and loneliness in the process. The process of recovery may, in fact, be long and drawn out. Time may creep to no apparent purpose. Those who grieve may wonder whether renewal is possible at all and whether the experiencing of the moments which we call time is even worth the effort.

THE SLOW PACE OF RENEWAL

The one object of grief is renewal, and one of its principles is the temporary changing of life's pace—a voluntary or involuntary slowing down so that the human spirit, wounded by the shock and loss, can catch up with the realities of the life it seeks to invigorate. Once it catches up, life can regain its momentum. Perhaps the meaning of time with respect to grief is here: the things that happen in our lives do not defeat us or wear us out, rather the pace with which we confront them does. We can move at a pace that kills or we can slow down to a contemplative peace that helps to renew us. We can charge furiously into life or we can retreat momentarily to be filled and renewed. Grief is nature's way of changing pace.

The chief reason that the process of grief is so

slow is that we do not understand it as we are passing through it. Clarity, no matter where it is found, always makes for greater speed; confusion makes for lack of toleration, energy, and decision. The larger picture of discernment comes into view only after many days of struggle, as the meaning of our misery slowly interprets our past and opens the door to the future. Early on, the whole story has not been told, or as Emerson phrased it: "The years teach much which the days never know."

The truth is that not many of us take inventory of our days, either to see how we are tending or where we have been. We leave it all, ironically, to New Year's Eve or to some other hapless occasion. But grief presses the point when life has fallen in upon us. It slows us to a sluggard's pace in which we begin to take inventory both of our past and of our future but only in light of what we are experiencing at the moment. In grief only the pain of the moment counts. Blaise Pascal (1623–1662), the great seventeenth century French scientist and religious philosopher, said it best of all:

> We never keep to the present. We recall the
> past; we anticipate the future as if we found it
> too slow in coming and were trying to hurry it
> up, or we recall the past as if to stay its too

rapid flight. We are so unwise that we wander about in times that do not belong to us, and do not think of the only one that does; so vain that we dream of times that are not and blindly flee the only one that is. The fact is that the present usually hurts. We thrust it out of sight because it distresses us, and if we find it enjoyable, we are sorry to see it slip away. We try to give it the support of the future, and think how we are going to arrange things over which we have no control for a time we can never be sure of reaching.[2]

Though our minds are busy "recalling the past" and "anticipating the future," the immediate pain is the only recognizeable stain with which we are all too up-to-date—but which we also detest. The endless thought-cycle from past to future to present tends to disarm us emotionally and rationally. C. S. Lewis kept a daily journal, "jottings" as he called it, of his inconsolable grief over the death of his wife, Joy Davidman. He wondered at a point whether or not the jottings were merely morbid—morbid perhaps because they seemed so pathetically disabling. He reflected the point we are making here when he wrote:

I once read the sentence "I lay awake all night with toothache, thinking about toothache and lying awake." That's true to life. Part of every misery is, so to speak, the misery's shadow or reflection: the fact that you don't merely suffer but have to keep on thinking about the fact that you suffer. *I not only live each day in grief, but live each day thinking about living each day in grief.*[3] (Italics added.)

As with Lewis, our whole world is taken up with the pain of the moment because we had a lovely past and are afraid that the future can never be the same again. The disturbing moments are fleeting; they never seem to accumulate so as to form a clear or settling picture of our lives; they only exchange places with one another, each maintaining the countenance of its own hurt and pain. And for all our understanding, hurt and pain only trudge, endlessly trudge.

Grief places us then in a state of passivity. This is true at least at the outset. We no longer bully our way through daily affairs with assurance. Because the road is unclear and its turns uncertain, we step, not with confidence but with caution. We take our time because time no longer greatly matters. Schedules offend us. Deadlines infuriate us. Our being on time somewhere gives way, unapologetically, to our untimely state of being. We march surefootedly to the beat of our own sense of need, yielding only guardedly to the next step.

37

There is a passage in *The Journal of John Woolman,* the great Quaker of early colonial America, in which he cites the precautionary nature of his own travels at a particularly fretful point in his life. He wrote: "I have gone forward, not as one travelling in a road cast up and well prepared, but as a man walking through a miry place in which are stones here and there safe to step on, but so situated that, one step being taken, time is necessary to see where to step next."[4]

In our grief, if we cannot place the stones upon which we hope to step, we at least want to find a pattern already laid, upon which we may safely pick our way forward. Therefore, grief becomes our own private journey as we decide the direction and dispatch of our very next step. The steps we ultimately take will help to define the shading of grief's slow stain upon our lives.

AN INVOLUNTARY SHADING

The shading of grief's slow stain upon our lives is largely involuntary. Much of its coloring takes place beneath the conscious level, so that we are not altogether in control of its impact. True to form, it drags us into a lot of places we would not normally find ourselves. We act in ways we would prefer not to act. We acquire feelings that are not native to us. Without our lifting a finger, it seems, our disposition takes on hues that are uncharacteristic of us and that, for the most part, become additions to our personalities against our protest.

Though we detest what is happening to us and even hate ourselves for being so passive and assenting, we are suffering under illusions which are not automatically apparent. When we look back upon our journey we will see how compliant were our choices and how absolutely discerning we would be, given the chance to make them again. To have such moments relived, we tell ourselves that we would take better charge of our lives, be less tolerant of depressive feelings, refuse to grovel in self-pity, or fall prey to abject loneliness. That is precisely what we would do, too, if we were already down the road to recovery. We know, however, that the precise lived-moment is our only valid experience, and that the choices cannot be brought back for correction. Our only option is to resist, in some manner, any further deluge.

Once we are aware of what grief is doing to us, we do not need to denigrate ourselves or throw character to the wind, for previously acquired character has everything to say about how grief affects our lives, and more-so how we are able to manage it. Our faith may be shaken, our theology questioned, our spiritual integrity threatened, and our ability to love God and to live life wisely temporarily jeopardized—but character established will eventually win the hour, like the breaking through of the sun on a cloudy day. Real character will rise to the surface such that, despite our being tested, we will come to affirm with the apostle Paul:

> We are hard pressed on every side, yet not crushed; we are perplexed, but not in despair; persecuted, but not forsaken; struck down, but not destroyed—always carrying about in the body the dying of the Lord Jesus, that the life of Jesus also may be manifested in our body.
> (2 Cor. 4:8–10)

We are often not even aware of how much real strength God has put into our character, until one day we find ourselves being tried in the fire. In the face of conflict and crisis we sometimes surprise ourselves.

During those early days and for several months following the loss of my best friend of twenty-eight years, no one could have convinced me that I would shuffle together the shattered pieces of such a personal loss and move on with unblinking confidence. How independent we were of one another, and yet how dependent we were upon one another's spirits! The emptiness of the road ahead rose up to meet me, and though the loss turned me topsy-turvy, it also challenged every fiber of my being. He was a dreamer, and we were dreamers together. I was resolved that this feature of our lives would not die in me. With the loss I realized how much character had been cut out in us as we had walked together. As I think about it even now, I find that it is character and character alone that makes us capable of facing and answering the interrogation of any sorrow.

Though we take on certain involuntary shading to our lives by the impact of grief upon them, we are also responsible for bringing to the situation the very best effort of which Christ has made us capable. He understands our initial shock and the momentary undermining of our strength, but he knows also the capacity of our character because it roots in his prevailing life. We have his assurance, as the apostle Peter reminds us:

> But may the God of all grace, who called us to His eternal glory by Christ Jesus, after you have suffered a while, perfect, establish, strengthen, and settle you. (1 Peter 5:10)

A TEMPORARY DYING BACK

Like the transplanting of a tender plant, grief transplants us into unproven soil, foreign to every fiber of our disposition. Like that succulent plant we die back, that is, we wilt or wither due to the shock of being uprooted. Some of our qualities are weakened. We forfeit some of our resiliency and actually lose ground for awhile before life begins to blossom forth again.

This dying back is a syndrome which nearly all experience to some degree. C. S. Lewis experienced a dying back, an early regression, if you will. The jottings which later became the book, were conserved briefly in eighty-nine pages. The first forty-seven pages are a willful confession of his doubts and even his rage against God, religion, and everything he held as the spiritual bulwark of his life. For half the book the reader listens to a pathetic man and pities him for his loss of faith in God and his absolute despair of life. Then, on page forty-eight, a giant of equally great spiritual proportions hails forth with the pronouncement: "I begin to see." On page fifty-one, "Something quite unexpected has happened"; on page fifty-two, "the lifting of sorrow removed a barrier"; on page fifty-three, "the door is no longer shut and bolted"; on page fifty-five, "I think I am beginning to under-stand. . . ." All the remaining pages depict a man who has rediscovered his faith in God, who finds recovery for his life, and who leaves the reader an endearing portrait of an honest man being consoled and consoling. Here is a classic of a man who had "died back" momentarily, until his roots in God rejuvenated to keep the plant alive, to put on new growth, and to recapture the vital-ity of the recovered life.

THE GIFT OF PATIENCE

We do not know what life and grief will make of us, ultimately. Certainly much of what we be-come will be due to what we make of ourselves and more especially what we allow God to make of us. If, to the contrary, we allow grief its own natural course, without our attempting to under-stand our own inner resources, we may be tempted to give out, give up, or give in to its whimpers of self-defeat. We must be ready, then, to find some realistic starting place to com-bat our desperate emotional inclination to give up.

From my own experience, along with what I gather from others who grieve, I know of only one starting place in the war against sorrow, and that is the gift of patience in the arms of Almighty God.

I recall here the experience of one of my former pastors, Dr. John Claypool, who lost his young daughter, Laura Lue, to leukemia. As Dr. Claypool watched his little daughter suffer, he could see no reason or purpose in what was happening to her. At that point he understood how a man could raise his hand against God, at times not far from doing so himself. At other times he suffered the temptation to despair as he felt like saying: "I quit. I give up. I can't stand it any longer. Stop the world. I want to get off." But his report was that he did not succumb to either temptation. The reason? Because the promise of Isaiah came true: "But those who wait for the LORD / Shall renew their strength; They shall mount up with wings like eagles, / They shall run and not be weary, / They shall walk and not faint" (Isa. 40:31). Claypool affirmed: "I was given the gift of patience, the gift of enduring. I was given the strength 'to walk and not faint'."[5]

The life of Dr. Claypool might have been stained negatively by grief. He might have become resentful toward God to the point of defiant rage. He might have cut himself off from life around him, becoming "shriveled and lifeless." But he did just the opposite. His relationship with God was an enabling one in which he *al-*

lowed God to be God. It reminds me of a brief limerick by the great teacher, W. O. Carver:

In hours of pain and grief
We learn in Him unfaltering faith and trust,
Only because we will and not because we must.[6]

Among the words that we heard from our pastor, Dr. Claypool, were these: "But if we are willing, the experience of grief can deepen and widen our ability to participate in life. We can become more grateful for the gifts we have been given, more open-handed in our handling of the events of life, more sensitive to the whole mysterious process of life, and more trusting in our adventure with God."[7]

When we ponder the capacity of grief's slow stain against the backdrop of our own, we realize that the journey may be prolonged—but we are encouraged when we hear Luke the physician saying to us: "In your patience possess your souls" (Luke 21:19). Consequently, as for our starting place in the journey through grief, I have only one exhortation, even as I exhort myself: *Be patient. God will outlast your sorrow.*

Getting through the Shadows

Lord,
I know that you take no pleasure in the
    suffering of your people.
        You desire only the best for us.
. . . .
Should you choose to intervene in such a way
    as to give me immediate relief,
        Let me never forget your goodness to me.
Should you choose not to intervene but rather
    to walk with me through the shadow,
        Give me the grace to know you are there!
                    —Creath Davis[1]

Nothing happens in our lives that does not involve other people—even tragedy. We are born into a shared life. But for the involvement of other people and their caring responsibility, we would never make it past our birth. If we are alive, then, we are vulnerable, and the threat never lessens. We will always need other people and even more so in the darkening hours of personal tragedy.

We may be thankful that the Judeo-Christian tradition has taught us this valuable lesson.

There is Someone who knows of our need of light because Sin and Death have made us creatures of darkness. There is Someone, also, to walk with us through the shadows: "I, the LORD your God, will hold your right hand . . . Fear not, I will help you." (Isa. 41:13); "Yea, though I walk through the valley of the shadow of death, I will fear no evil; For You are with me" (Ps. 23:4).

This *God of help* bonds the shared community of ancient Israel with the shared fellowship of Christianity, the new Israel. In the New Testament the word is *koinonia,* depicting the support of common life in a spiritual community of faith in God. The colony of God's people was no longer composed of Jew or Gentile. Paul said that the middle wall of division that had divided the two had, in Christ, been broken down and that the new generic was now a "bodied-together" people (Eph. 2:14–15).

A shared community means different things to different people. At the base, however, the New Testament community depicts a fellowship of shared life in a vital way. Involvement with others, caring responsibility, real servanthood, and *vulnerability* in a positive, healing fashion became the overtones of the group in the midst of an age of persecution. Life was shared both from the perspective of its successes and its failures, from the posture of its triumphs and its tragedies. The little community had often to meet just to bind up her wounds and to soften the blow of social and political defeat. Though they became isolated, they lost neither their verve nor their vitality, because they had each other and Christ as their supreme model for overcoming. Consequently, they became *enablers* and *encouragers* to one another in their common journey.

When the lights dim across our pathway, we also must bind our hearts more intimately than ever before. How desperately we need each other when the shadows fall.

SHADOWS OF PAIN

Shadows aptly describe the passageway through which we move in our journey through grief. Mentally, perhaps even spiritually, everything seems hazy, fuzzy, dim, if not altogether dark. The intense pain, the feeling of loss isolates us, makes us doubt our own sanity. We need help, especially from those loving persons who so boldly dare to enter our lives at the point of our pain and to share vicariously our tears and hurt.

Pain, like people, casts its own peculiar

shadow. Your pain is different from my pain just as the shadow you cast is different from mine. Among the many inventions of Thomas Jefferson was a silhouette machine. Only by use of this interesting little gadget could one draw his own shadow. The drawback of using the machine, however, is that the completed silhouette is only a miniature, good for framing and hanging on a wall. The shadow cast by our pain, however, is always life-size, and no machine can bring that anguish down to manageable size. How difficult it is, also, to stand tall in our hurt and at the same time reach out far enough to trace the shadow that it casts; hence to understand our trying condition.

The point is that we cannot always be *objective* with our own pain. We often do not understand it nor more often have the capacity to bear it alone. In our experience with grief and anguish, we desperately need someone to help us *see through it* as well as to help us *see it through*. Though it is our own pain and misery, we need the loving touch of someone alongside us who can trace the silhouette for us. And although we wish they could erase the entire shadow, only we ourselves have that prerogative.

The cry for a supportive fellowship, then, is not an option, but a necessity. But those who would help us must be totally different from the help afforded Job by his friends. They wanted to help Job explain his misery; but grief explained is not thereby grief softened. The objective guidance of any fellowship should be explanatory and directive only to the extent that it has experienced a similar pain. A blind man who wants to get from one place to another may tolerate the leadership of one who can see clearly the way to go. But if he wants someone to fully *understand* his blindness he will trust only the "views" of those who are blind like himself.

In the recent loss of my best friend of twenty-eight years, there have been times when I miss grievously the fellowship and comradery we knew. At times I have caught myself wishing I could just call him on the telephone to share my latest ventures, to talk over old adventures, and to design new ones together, as we did for so many years. Each time, I experience the deep loss—he is no longer there as before. No one has to tell me how sensitive the pain is, though there may be plenty of persons in our fellowship who could well say, "I know precisely how you feel."

Yet, knowing my level of loss and pain, I can go only so far in trying to be a comfort to his wife. Comparing it to mine, I can only *imagine* how deep is her loss, because our experiences are not the same. To a great extent, he was her life, so special was their unity. The fact that I cannot understand the depth of her loss fully does not prevent my wanting to share the loss in some supportive way. It is good that I cannot *answer her questions;* it is even better that, given the same need for fellowship and care, I can at least *quest with her for the answers.* I can only dimly help her see through the shadows, but I can commit myself totally for as long as it takes to help her see the shadows through. There is a vast difference, indeed.

SUPPORT IN THE SHADOWS

How does a fellowship, then, help the grief-stricken through the shadows? In what ways are the clouds driven away so that the sunlight may shine through again?

The Gift of Time

Grieving persons need for us to give the *gift of time.* We can be present, but we dare not be pushy. We must never forget that grief is a journey which must be traveled at each individual's own pace. Coping is important; however, the pace is determined not by our own inconvenience but the journey of the traveler. Our insensitive question, "When will you ever be able to cope?" is unwarranted. If they knew the answer to that question, they would no longer be on the journey, looking for new roads to recovery, checking out new signposts for direction, trying desperately to find their way again.

Time in itself is not a *healer;* it is only a *revealer* in the way. The process of healing begins with revelations. The more insightful those revelations, the more rapidly we move in the process. How grateful we are in our grief, when those next to us say, "Please, take all the time you need." When a fellowship can do that for us, amazingly the healing process takes much less time than first imagined.

Encouragers from Depression

Emotional depression short-circuits our feeling capacity, creates a sort of numbness, and distorts our mental vision. This is why grief changes the healthy channels of our own sane perspective of things and leaves us groping through a mental fog. Sometimes we get so far off the beaten trail that professional help is necessary to direct us back onto the path of reality. Of course, there is to be absolutely no shame for requiring this service; it simply tells us that, for the moment, we need supportive guidance more than our friends can offer. Sensitive is the friend who can see our plight and direct us to the proper source of help.

Depression, due to loss, creates an aimlessness that even undercuts our feelings of faith. Our faith in ourselves is distorted. Self-confidence easily goes out the window. Gratefully, the forcefulness of our depression leaves us seeking outside ourselves. We find ourselves needing to put our faith in another for the restoration of our own self-confidence. Hence, our need of an inner circle of friends who understand us, our need of a close fellowship, an intimate community and, yes, a recommitment to trust in the Christ of our journey. Through the shadows he becomes, again, the true vision of our daily walk. He, as well as those committed to him, become our encouragers from depression, those who are capable of helping us dissipate the darkness.

Depression may be defined in many ways because it has many roots and many symptoms, but when it comes to the bombardment of grief, depression is at heart "hope deferred." At the most hopeless point in grieving is the deepest depression. Absolute hopelessness is utter despair, the ultimate expression of depression.

Depression harbored inordinately will subsequently lead to emotional sickness. When things seem hopeless, and all desire leaves us, the life goes out of us, too. We seem sick unto death, healthless, pallid, and washed out. Depression is as the Bible defines it, "Hope deferred makes the heart sick, but when the desire comes, it is a tree of life" (Prov. 13:12).

Pain can be a gift if it awakens us to the reality of hope instead of forcing us into depression. We regain hope only if we allow the pain to transform us instead of letting it defeat us. Part of our pain, and subsequently our depression, comes because we feel alone. If we are not cautious, that aloneness will degenerate into self-centered pity, the most damaging characteristic of depression.

If, instead, we can recognize the pain that we must endure as wind in our sails, we will *use* the agony rather than *curse* it. The using of it can stimulate hope. It can actually dredge up for us a resiliency and strength that we did not know we had. When we look long and hard at pain we begin to see it not as something pushing us or beating at us but as something challenging us and calling us to creativity. In this sense, pain is a gift, an invitation to look at our own incompleteness in the light of God's transcending purpose for our lives.

If we were the only beings in the universe, emotional pain would not exist. The very nature of this pain comes from our having been intimately related with at least one other being like ourselves, and then having that relationship severed. Our consolation comes, not in knowing the origin of our grief, but that its presence assures us there was love and, therefore, life.

Depression is then, ultimately, the giving in to pain. *Hope regained,* or the antithesis of depression, is the confronting of that pain and the adventurous return to life—especially the return to a life with others. We are driven from an aloneness by our own need of other people. Out of the shared pain comes a reuniting with those who shared it, and we become, in turn, enablers of their hope as well as our own. We become as Nouwen has phrased it, "wounded healers."

Obviously, those who are wounded become the best servants of hope. Unless pain is permitted to transform the vision of our hearts, we will miss our place in the ministry of hope. If we do not become encouragers in return, we know at least one thing: our pain has missed its purpose.

Shared Loneliness

We cannot give our loneliness to another, nor can another take away our loneliness. Support from others in our lonely journey is a real and treasured boon to our lives, but no one can travel down the road of our own wounds for us. Others only help us to recognize the reality of our loneliness and ultimately to discover the meaning of that solitude by the affirmation of their presence. They never really heal us, for that is an impossibility, but their corroboration with our aching spirits is like the lifting of a heavy burden or the suturing of a mortal wound.

The existentialist, Sartre, was plainly remiss in saying that "Hell is other people." If that is true, then we are in deeper trouble than we ever presumed ourselves to be. Certainly, there are times when we cherish our privacy, and times when "other people" are bothersome or overbearing, just as each of us has had his share of being annoying. But where do we turn when the going gets tough or when we perceive our loneliness. Precisely, we look for "other people" to whom we may tell our story. And is it not strange to avow that God would create his own hell by creating "other people"? Again, why would he state that "it is not good that man should be alone," if He did not see the practical enrichment implicit in "other people"? Would Adam have done just as well skipping through life solo? What Sartre failed to discern in the basic condition of man is the reality of how utterly dependent he is, which includes Sartre himself!

Our feelings of aloneness and alienation, if not distorted, will drive us into a unity with other beings. Such unity must happen if we are to convert our depressive loneliness into a newly creative functioning in life. The creative joy of life demands the constancy of personal encounter. The recluse of no purpose dies in his loneliness.

In our *solitude,* when we are alone with our thoughts, we feel our *loneliness* the most. But the hope of every Christian fellowship, where the drama of joy and grief unite, is that someone struggling alone will find a comforting firelight for the shadows of their lonely days and nights. If, for the moment, we can be sure that someone is with us in our loneliness, we can enter our solitude less afraid.

New Direction

Out of a supportive community, also, comes new direction amid the shadows. Decisions come hard when one is alone and even harder if one is alone in his suffering. A fellowship of people who share the concerns of the sufferer help to open new doors possibly gone unnoticed by those engrossed in their pain.

Though most of us want the privilege of making our own decisions, we know that we very seldom make major ones without consulting someone else. In times of grief especially we need guidance. All along the journey we pass sideroads and wonder whether or not we should divert our course onto one of them. Perhaps someone else knows where they lead. Perhaps someone else will travel partway with us until we are sure of the next turns in the road.

In his book, *Loneliness and Love,* Clark E. Moustakas points out that "man strives for new directions; he seeks to find vitality and excitement, and as he does he awakens to new images; the old patterns and bonds are broken."[2] Moustakas then shares some of his own inner struggles for truth and meaning, depicting himself as someone in search of a realistic light and a path that does not turn out to be a mere fantasy, hoping that the next step he takes is real, that his heartbeat is his own.

In his "hours alone" the possibility of coming to know himself again and the ability to return to real life is a genuine mode of recovery. Then he adds:

> But while a person is struggling in lonely silence to find his way back to life again, to give birth to a new path that comes from within, to restore his spirit and passion for life, he needs strong, unqualified, affirming voices; he needs to avoid rejecting people, tentative people, and the "yes-but" people who surround him. Only the totally affirming, spontaneous, and unreserved can help him in this struggle and give him the

courage and strength to return alone to his thoughts and feelings. Only they can help him discover what he really wants to do, and with whom he can take this journey.[3]

We are inextricably tied to one another's lives. We need each other in the present shock of our past hurt, and we need each other in the challenge of tomorrow. Changes have to be made: our intimate losses demand it; our own sanity requires it; the music of past relationships haunts us longingly and must find repose. The climate of other people is the hotbed where these changes can be rooted until, like delicate seedlings, they can be safely transplanted into life at large and have the enlarged space to flourish and blossom. The fellowship, then, becomes God's intended hothouse to make *new starts* in life not only possible but adventurous.

Henri J. M. Nouwen put it quite succinctly when he wrote:

. . .It is in common searches and shared risks that new ideas are born, that new visions reveal themselves and that new roads become visible.

We do not know where we will be two, ten or twenty years from now. What we can know, however, is that man suffers and that a sharing of suffering can make us move forward.[4]

Even when we have been equipped by great teachers and have become relatively self-directed in life, we still need the corroboration of others. Perhaps we feel the need of a checks-and-balances support as a security measure against our own sense of prowess and adequacy. To a large extent our security rests in the affirmation we receive from other people. Our security level is threatened when we receive rejection of any kind. No matter how secure we may feel inwardly, when we are suffering anguish, we certainly need confirmation of love from someone. The decisions we make and the directions we take depend upon it more than we know.

The greatest tragedy of our lives would be that in the pain of our loss we had to, also, go looking for love. Thank God that in the security of a likeminded fellowship, love comes to us when we need it the most. If we can be sure of love, we can be sure of life, whatever direction it takes, even if it takes us through the shadows.

How to Win over Loneliness

We must face grief without any expectation of
miraculous healing, but with the knowledge that
if we are courageous and resolute we can live
as our loved ones would wish us to live, not
empty, morose, self-centered, and self-pitying,
but as brave and undismayed servants of the
greater life.

—Joshua Loth Liebman[1]

Only five months after the death of my best
friend, Creath Davis, I was thrown into a setting
that had been for years familiar ground for both
of us. Memories raced through my mind to ig-
nite an almost fever of depression. To any telling
degree the shadows had not lifted for me.

The familiar ground was the site of our tenth
annual deer and turkey hunt, with a group of
men. Most of us that first day merely met the
schedule by rote, our real reason for being
there, largely unspoken. By mealtime, I was unable to voice our prayer over the meal, so I asked
another dear friend of Creath's, Dick Sayles, a
lawyer in our group, if he would express our
thanks. None of us were embarrassed as he

tried, and we tried with him, choking back our feelings of loss. We enjoyed the meal and the fellowship, but not as before.

That evening, Creath's eldest son, David, came to my room. For two hours we talked about the plane crash that took his father's life. We shared our feelings, we shook our heads disbelievingly, we questioned ourselves, we questioned God, we questioned life, and then questioned our questions. Though we sensed a mutual support, we still felt our grief was unassauged, and we parted, having settled very little.

The next day was the day that Creath and I usually spent the afternoon hunting together. Actually, we did very little hunting; we often wound up in a blind together talking. We served as each other's counselors, talked of our dreams, or tried our latest thoughts on one another. We laughed a lot and, were the truth known, the wild game probably laughed more than we did. Under normal conditions one must remain extremely still if he expects the game to show themselves, especially the wily West Texas turkey tom. On one occasion, however, the two of us were enjoying rather boisterously our usual camaraderie when to our astonishment an entire group of turkeys walked up totally oblivious of our presence; whereupon, we promptly took our rifles and bagged a nice tom for our day's effortlessness.

This particular afternoon was to be patently different. Most of the men on the hunt had told me earlier in the day that they planned to return home following the afternoon hunt. I had planned to remain through the next day. I spent the afternoon muddling through the hunt, thinking mostly about the previous years of companionship with my friend. It struck me that for the first time in twenty-eight years, including all the hunts that we had shared together, I was *alone* in the field. Never in my life had I felt such aloneness. I drove back to the camp knowing that no one would be there, including Creath, thinking back over our spiritual ventures together, hurting over the great loss to his family, wondering where the road would lead from here. For the first time in my life I was experiencing deeply the meaning of depressed loneliness.

Somehow it came to me that if I could come to grips with myself and deal with this depressed mood, I might determine what God intended for the remainder of *my* life. Someone had to pick up where the two of us left off; and I was not having any doubts as to what that meant. Momentarily, I avowed that I would give it the best shot I could muster, God being my helper. I thanked God that I had had the gift of a friend for all those years, then driving down the road to camp, I sang awhile and cried awhile, and tried to dream as the two of us had done so many times before; only now I was doing it without the benefit of our close fellowship.

The symptoms of loneliness are many-sided. Loneliness during grief comes from many grieving moods and takes on the emotional shading characteristic of those moods.

MENTAL LONELINESS

Sometimes we are (as I experienced in the field) alone in our *confusion*. In this sense, loneliness is a kind of lostness, a kind of uprootedness; at least the feeling is experienced as loneliness, because in every way we feel cut off.

Death itself confuses us about life and meaning. We long for answers to questions with which we have never had to contend. We grieve not only for our losses but for not having solutions to the emptiness we feel. Confused in so many ways, we drive inward and still find ourselves alone. We have difficulty interpreting our muddled condition and putting a label on it. So, our confusion becomes a kind of mental loneliness as we live through segments of life for which we have no clear understanding. Numbed by our pain we are unable to penetrate into the inner recesses of our souls and instead grovel on the outside of ourselves where meaning seems to be lost.

This disarray becomes the underlying confusion that we describe as a "mental fog" when we are faced with great loss. All that is apparent to us about "fog" in any setting is that it is aimless, rootless, and vague. That is precisely how we feel, compounded by our feeling of isolation in it. As Seneca questioned: "To whom can any man say—'Here I am! Behold me in my nakedness, my wounds, my secret grief, my despair, my betrayal, my pain, my tongue which cannot express my sorrow, my terror, my abandonment.'"

LONELINESS AND ANXIETY

Some loneliness, moreover, comes from *anxiety* incurred during times of grief. Certain fears and anxieties arise in the face of our loss such as the drive to look inward. When we are forced into an undesirable state of isolation, we are vividly aware that we are no longer the same person. If we have lost a mate in death, we have lost more than a mate; we have lost an *identity*. For so long we knew ourselves as part of someone else, and someone else was part of us. Now we are lost, uncentered human beings. Old connections and bonds have been broken, and now we are involuntarily driven into the deep of ourselves to discern who we really are.

The barrenness of this responsibility is extremely unappealing to us. An actual fearfulness is present in this *isolation of identity*. We are afraid of what we may find when we look within. We question the genuineness and reality of our lives; we face momentarily the discerning of our destiny alone. Our fear, as well as the loneliness it precipitates, immobilizes us and we stand in a lonely stalemate with ourselves. We dread the inevitable dialogue with ourselves; we are not sure that we can handle the solitude that makes us face ourselves. Are we really certain that we want to know ourselves apart from the one we loved?

This fearfulness of facing ourselves is not unlike our fearfulness toward those around us; and the loneliness that we experience in our own inwardly grieving journey is not unlike our outward loneliness as we cut ourselves off from other people. Paul Tournier, in fact, points out that "men's loneliness is linked with fear. Men fear one another, fear to be crushed in life, fear to be misunderstood. . . . Fear breeds loneliness and conflict; loneliness and conflict breed fear. To heal the world, we must give men an answer to fear and restore among them the sense of community."[2]

LONELINESS AND DEPRESSION

A third form of loneliness is that characterized by *depression*.

Our most damaging experience is not the depression itself but our response or reaction toward it, for example, self-pity. As Liebman has pointed out, sometimes our mourning is really a mourning for ourselves, an expression of self-centered pity for our own directionless lives.[3]

From a psychological and social standpoint, in the early stages of our grief, we naturally become the center of our world. At such a time no one would dare begrudge us an intensity of individual attention from those who care for us deeply. But there will come a day when gradually, naturally, and meaningfully, we begin to allow the needs and concerns of others to filter back into our world. With some predominant force we return again to an other-centered approach to life. How long it takes for this to occur is not important; what is important is its occurrence. We will actually benefit ourselves psychologically as we begin to meet needs outside ourselves. Now, rather than hearing no other voice except our own raised in self-pity, we will declare a realistic concern for the rest of life around us.

There were times when even Christ himself sensed a feeling of loneliness, but he never wallowed in it. The next scene always shows him reaching out beyond himself, and that cured his melancholia. This response always gave him back his sense of dignity and kept him from self-pity. We must know that we are worth something to someone else, or we will bask in our own self-pity, endless depression, and loneliness.

LONELINESS AND GUILT

In the fourth place, how many there are who experience a *loneliness of guilt,* and who suffer in silence with feelings that cannot be comfortably aired. The repression of guilt feelings, however, only drives one into a deeper loneliness and opens the door to emotional illness.

A lady who had recently lost her husband was once referred to me by a colleague for counseling. Whereas she had always been a deeply religious person, she expressed to her family a growing bitterness toward God. Her depression was far and beyond the normal amount experienced by grieving persons, and included some frightening hallucinations. Our consultations and testing revealed among other things the presence of guilt, self-pity and feelings of victimization. An internalizing of stress (in this case guilt) was contributing to various physical reactions. An indirect expression of hostility was also likely. Her depression was of an acute reactive type, related to her husband's death.

She repeatedly expressed her bitterness toward God, and I wondered why she, a very religious person, had suddenly turned on the object of her faith with such harshness. Combining this with strong remarks in reference to her deceased husband, I sensed that she was not angry with God at all, but, in fact, with her spouse. Her transfer of anger upon God indirectly was more acceptable to her than admitting to her family misgivings toward her husband whom she really loved.

By mental suggestion, I took her back to the day of her husband's death and to the room where he had died.

"Is Jesus there in the room?" I asked.

"Yes. He is smiling and reaching out to me."

"What is he saying to you?"

"He is saying, 'I love you. I am here to be with you.'"

She had previously told me that she had not felt God's presence on the day of her husband's death. And now only in response to my reconstructing the scene for her was she able to visualize the kind of God she had always loved. The basis for continued bitterness toward him was gone.

When we broke the mental suggestion and returned to our consultation, I asked her what she was feeling toward her deceased husband. "I know I shouldn't," she responded, "but I feel angry with him—angry for leaving me so depleted and disorganized financially." She related how he had left large outstanding bills relating to his company, the relinquishment of which took almost all of the life insurance benefits that had come to her. In actuality, she was grieving the loss of her mate, as well as struggling desperately to make ends meet. On top of her grief and desperation she was feeling guilty for her unresolved bitter feelings. She was in turn driven into a deep sense of loneliness because she could not tell her family what was really troubling her. Her suffering in silence caused dangerous emotional and physical symptoms.

Following this session, this very charming person began to lose her depressed moods, her hallucinations, and certain associated physical complaints. During our final session together she asked, "What have you done to me in such a short time to bring back my old personality?"

Obviously, I had done nothing but to help her deal with guilt feelings that she suffered alone. Dredged up from the depths of her, forgiven and understood, her guilt and anger left her. She had entered again the circle of love and felt her old acceptable personality returning.

AN OVERBURDENED CONSCIENCE

A fifth reaction is what may be termed the *loneliness of an overburdened conscience*. This reaction is especially focal in the loss of the family's breadwinner. Problems arise, and heavy responsibilities aggravate. The tiring reorganization and restructuring of daily affairs takes its toll, and making decisions becomes the loneliest responsibility of all, unless someone can guide us to the required determinations.

No one can heal his spirit whose conscience is weighted down beyond his capacity to organize at the moment. Retreating from time to time is advisable, but only if such is observed as a much-needed solitude and not a shirking of matters that only we can resolve.

This aspect of loneliness is especially grinding for the aging person. Age takes its toll naturally with the loss of a lifetime companion, but the loss of certain functional capacities compounds the difficulty of every effort. Feelings of uselessness also burden the conscience of the aging, not to mention feelings of one's getting in the way or interrupting the social lives of younger and more functional friends and family. The empty house is possibly emptier to the aging, because the need for companionship is merged with basic physical needs. When the spirit is still agile and adventurous but the body becomes sluggish, aged persons find themselves more remote and alone. These features of life under duress and grief are seemingly more overbearing than that afflicting the younger generation. A truly great Christian ministry is the ministry to the aged, especially when they experience the loss of someone dear.

LONELINESS AND LOSS

We must not omit the most obvious mood swings of all—the loneliness of loss itself. Nothing is quite as lonely as losing a loving, joyful and fulfilling relationship. This loss may be due to death of a partner or an unwanted divorce. And many other losses over which persons grieve could be named as well.

In the death of a mate, we know full well the *reason* for our grief that registers as loneliness. We have lost a presence that meant everything to us. A dear friend who recently lost her husband said to me, "I am not lonely *for myself,* but I am lonely *for him.*" Though on the surface such a remark sounds contradictory, a knowledge of this couple's past relationship along with her values and purpose in life makes the remark qualitatively clear. Another close friend, when asked what she wanted, replied, "I just want him back!"

Psychological loneliness, existential loneliness, personal loneliness—however we want to categorize or define the feeling—all come down to one issue: the loss of someone who made our lives joyful and complete.

Loneliness, at root, is ever a "longing for union," but that observation is too philosophical, too erudite, too nebulous. In grief, loneliness is plainly *the longing for a lost union that can never be regained.* The *meaning* is not lost, but the most cherished union of our lives has been taken from us, and we are alone because of it. The feeling itself must be its own definition, because no words are adequate to describe it. What is unmistakably clear is that this "loneliness" makes us its objective, causing the person to turn inward, becoming introspective, and even

73

self-centered. Perhaps the true force of loneliness is resident in the title of a well-known country and western song: "The Last Word in Lones*ome* is Me" (italics added).

How, then, are we to win over any one or all of these forms of loneliness? We must know that there is a solution, or at least steps in that direction.

A CHANGE OF ATTITUDE

Somewhere along the journey through grief we eventually sense that no amount of tears and sorrow will change the *fact of loss*. Our only real option is to change our attitude toward it. Accordingly, we must place our best effort in that direction. No amount of effort will change the *reason* of our grief and loneliness; only our reaching for meaning that changes us will suffice.

We may have "lost" (if that is the proper word here) a great portion of our sense of meaning when we lost our beloved, but at that we have not been deprived of meaning itself. The meaning that we experienced in the past can never be lost because our past is eternal. The present and the future are only on the threshold of the eternal; they become part of the eternal only as they become part of the past.

In order to understand a continuing meaning we need to understand the logic of time. The following syllogism seems clear: The eternal does not change, for if it does, it is not eternal but transitory. The past is unchangeable. Therefore, the past is eternal.

Though the past is unchangeable, it is *real* in the present moment because of its *memory* and *meaning*. These are the only two features that comprise past experience—memory and meaning. But the past's meaning alone makes it eternal. Its meaning will prevail long after we are incapable of recalling it, say, in the event of our own death. This is why the Germans have two words for "history": *historie,* the factual events themselves, and *geschichte,* the meaning of those events.

The *union* that once existed no longer exists, but the *unity* that we experienced in that union does. That unity meant something rich and wondrous to us and it still does—and it always will; it is eternal and in that sense changeless, except in growing quality. In dealing with our loneliness, the real question to ask ourselves about our loss is not "Does it have meaning?" but "What is its meaning for us now?"

We cannot change our past; we must allow our past to change us or we must change ourselves in relation to it. We may have the *right* to be lonely because we have the *reason* to be, but if we are bent on maintaining that right we have made a fatal mistake. We can go on clinging to the attitude of the will-to-loneliness and it will kill us, or we can change our attitude to the will-to-meaning and it will change the nature of our loneliness and eventually enrich our lives. We must do more than merely adjust to the reality of our loss; we must make something of it!

LONELINESS AND SOLITUDE

The place to do something valuable with our loneliness is in our *solitude*. When we come right down to it, in our *solitude*, when we are alone with our thoughts, we feel our loneliness most. We feel cut off from the concern and support of others who may also understand us in our misery. So easily do we become overly dependent upon others. What is vital, however, is the courage of being alone where the restructuring of our lives can form on the basis of our most intimate feelings about ourselves.

Paul Tournier described one side of the coin of solitude-and-fellowship when he wrote: "It may be that the deeper experience of fellowship has as one of its necessary conditions that we first achieve a creative solitude."[4] Still, only fellowship with some sensitive, caring person permits us into the intimate inner feelings, to focus and thereby to resolve our own loneliness. People who meet us in our loneliness give us the encounter that we need to make our solitude creative. As Tournier has pointed out, we must possess communion with ourselves before we can be in communion with others, but also our intimacy with others drives us into the richest aspects of our own being. Caring people, without a doubt, give us courage and faith in ourselves to face ourselves creatively in our solitude.

Solitude serves two purposes: it is for *reflection* and *healing*.

First, solitude is the positive side of our loneliness in which we contemplate and meditate upon the meaning and hope left in our lives. We reflect upon our need of God and his desire for us. We open our lives to *receive* the meaning that only God can adequately help us to discover in ourselves. Once we know that hope we are ready to *give* meaning to the world.

Secondly, solitude is for healing. In solitude we suture and dress our wounds. We come before God for understanding of ourselves and for perceiving new directions. And if we follow the example of Jesus Christ, that may at times mean our praying all night (Luke 6:12–13). Little by little we give our wounds to the Wounded Healer, because we know that he alone knows the extent of our struggle. "And by His stripes we are healed" (Isa. 53:5).

LONELINESS AND LOVE

This brings us to one of the richest sources for resolving our loneliness—the overriding need to *receive* and *give* ourselves in love.

To cure our loneliness we must first be receptive to all the love experienced in our past. This does not mean some dismal tying of ourselves to what we can no longer hold of our past. A ruthless clinging to our past in an effort to maintain it as we know it, for instance, is not only hopeless but dangerous. In our grief we can so easily become fixated personalities. On the other hand, to know that in our past we loved and were loved by one whom we have now lost in death can be consoling because of the rich meaning that flooded our lives. If we do not cherish *now* the indescribable meaning that was ours *then,* then the very thought of our past will drive us even more desperately into loneliness.

Viktor Frankl, the eminent psychiatrist of Vienna who spent the war years imprisoned by the Nazis both at Auschwitz and Dachau, speaks of this need to contemplate past meanings, especially those that emanate from past affections. In the concentration camp at Dachau, Frankl found himself imagining the presence of his wife, envisaging her in his memories, and in his mind speaking with her and hearing her respond. This seemed at least a temporary reprieve of his suffering. He would later write in *Man's Search For Meaning:*

> In a position of utter desolation, when man cannot express himself in positive action, when his only achievement may consist in enduring his sufferings in the right way—an honorable way—in such a position man can, through loving contemplation of the image he carries of his beloved, achieve fulfillment.[5]

After much suffering in the bitter cold of the labor camp in which the prisoners worked ill-clothed, sick and hungry, Frankl continued his recollections:

> My mind still clung to the image of my wife. A thought crossed my mind: I didn't even know if she were still alive. I knew only one thing—

which I have learned well by now: Love goes very far beyond the physical person of the beloved. It finds its deepest meaning in his spiritual being, his inner self. Whether or not he is actually present, whether or not he is still alive at all, ceases somehow to be of importance.[6]

We can continue the healing of our loneliness as we begin, in our own way, to complete the legacy of those whom we loved. By this is not meant assuming their precise role, so much as the principles, dreams, and concerns that gripped their lives. As Liebman clarifies it:

We must act as the ambassadors of our departed, their messengers and their spokesmen, carrying out the mission for which they lived and strove and which they bequeathed to us. They lived, they toiled, they laughed, they served, and we must be their worthy emissaries in the portion of life that they leave behind them.[7]

This assumption of a legacy is a special way of using the love that we have received. In this we teach ourselves and demonstrate to the world that love does not die.

Not only must we receive the love of our past but of our present social surrounding, as well. In spite of our loneliness, if not because of it, we must continue to enter the circle of love by receiving the love of other people. Most of our current relationships are nurturing to us rather than overbearing. To deny those relationships a place in our suffering is to invite a loneliness that emanates from our own self-imposed emptiness. We are as rich or as poor in meaning as our relationships. This is why loneliness, at its most burdensome point, occurs when one feels alienated or cut off from love. A reuniting with love is of utmost necessity.

Finally, the richest source of healing our loneliness is for us to begin to give ourselves in love. Granted, we must recover from our initial pain and find a measure of healing for our own souls before we will feel much like offering our lives to others. At a proper moment, however, we will rediscover the principle of our own fulfillment, one that also will ultimately dispel our loneliness. That principle is a reaching out to a need to be filled. Until we move outside ourselves and focus outward toward others, we will continue to be empty, self-pitying, lonely human beings. This will be true whether we are grieving some loss or residing in some ivory tower untouched by human heartbreak.

At base man must give himself away or remain pathetically empty and alone. This elevation of oneself by giving oneself away is the very root and life blood of being human. When man cannot so order his life but instead turns inward, he ceases to grow and to be fulfilled. To the contrary, he must forget himself, at least in the self-centered sense, and give himself for the sole sake of someone else. There is no transcendence greater.

Only by adopting the kind of love that can be given away can we become, as Liebman states in the epigraph that heads this chapter—"brave and undismayed servants of the greater life." Unless we do become servants at large, seeking out needs like our own to be filled, we will become Liebman's other caricature: "empty, morose, self-centered, and self-pitying" human beings. What a victory is ours, only to know that serving love will dispel almost any gloom!

What to Do with the Hurt

Let us draw near with a true heart in full assurance of faith . . . . Let us hold fast the confession of our hope without wavering, for He who promised is faithful.

—Hebrews 10:22,-23

Very early in my ministry I was the pastor of a rural church which, although it contained a few young families, was by-and-large composed of older adults. As a natural course, death came to the aging in this small community church more often than with similar churches composed of the younger generations. As a result, I spent a lot of time presiding at memorial services.

The death of one of the longtime members of this church, a well-loved deacon, was especially hard for all who knew him. I had an especially rich relationship with this dear friend—and a friend he was, indeed, to everyone. There is nothing he would not do for anyone in the community regardless of expense to himself, either in time or money. He was a true servant of God who radiated joy and love, whose death raised a lot of questions about the purpose and work of God in our lives.

I recall sitting down at the little breakfast table with his wife, where on many occasions the three of us had discussed together the great questions and concerns of our faith, as well as the everyday joys of our lives. This particular morning she raised the inevitable question, "*Why* does this have to happen to me?" She went on qualifying her sincere reasons for her feelings of loss and hurt, but she kept returning to her original question: "Why?"

THE REAL QUESTION

At the time, I had been pastoring only three years and was not especially versed in answering such monumental questions. But God supplied a sincere response then that I think holds true to this day. I said to her, "Mrs. Adams, I know that your asking 'why' is a legitimate question and it deserves an answer in time, but the real question that you are asking at this point is 'how?'— 'How am I going to get through this?'" After some discussion, she agreed.

In every setting of bereavement the initial question is the same—"*How* will I ever get through the hurt?" Obviously, we will wrestle with our grief, try to understand it, perhaps seek to bear it boldly, even attempt to deal with it responsibly. Or we may react in an opposite manner. We may bring to the hurt our anger, our bitterness, and even our reactions of despair and futility.

In our very worst moments, we stop and ask ourselves, "What is it all for?" This is the question, we recall, of Ernie Pyle, the average American G.I., a World War II correspondent on the frontlines of battle. Word reached him there of the death of his mother. Alone, he struggled with the ultimate question of the meaning of life but found no answers. Falling back upon his writing, he recorded his reactions in these poignant words: "It seems to me that life is futile and death the final indignity. People live and suffer and grow bent with yearning, bowed with disappointment, and then they die. And what is it all for? I do not know."

In our suffering and hurt we ask the same questions—"What is it all for?"; "Why does this happen to me?" This is natural, largely because we are not our true selves, and are not expected to be, during such times of stress and disorientation. Even the biblical Job's wife, in the face of all his seeming futility, retorted: "Curse God and die!" (Job 2:9). Certainly, there are occasions when the hurt penetrates so deeply that we almost despair and even wish that God would take us to be with him. In our lolling spirit, however, we are not able to discern at the moment that such a resignation may be purely selfish.

Of course, when we are hurting desperately, we are at our most vulnerable stage. We are our world, and that is about as far as we can see at the moment. If others know how vulnerable we are and overlook our self-centeredness, we are grateful. They kindly wait for us to become ourselves again. What a boon to our healing!

For certain, we will bring to our hurt some kind of response or reaction. Apart from total insanity, in which case we are incapable of a proper response, hurt is too strong a threat for us to be indifferent toward it. A man may appear stoical about his pain and make every effort to deny its reality. He only fools himself, however, because everyone knows that hiding one's head in the sand like the proverbial ostrich does not detach one from life around him. The ostrich only hides his head; the remainder of him is totally vulnerable.

Suppressed and even repressed pain is really not a removal of it. The pain is still there, taking on different forms, producing other more damaging symptoms, without relieving the real pain. Indifference to hurt is a response of a sort, but a very poor one.

How, then, are we going to deal with our hurt *personally?* As Christians, we want a decisively spiritual answer whatever else it may be. We often go to the New Testament hoping to find the formula set out in simple, practical, logical, and numerical succession. Except for a number of cherished isolated scriptures that have always given us comfort, we find our search for the *precise formula* for facing grief largely missing. I have questioned many times why the New Testament writers did not include any precise "episodes of grief" and how we are to deal with the pain in a practical manner. There are no specific dialogues of Christ with people regarding their sorrow. Oh, he worked miracles in the presence of sickness and death in which immediate joy was restored. Certainly, he showed concern and care in the presence of distress and grief— Lazarus's sisters, the widow of Nain, the Syro-Phoenician woman, the Roman Centurion, and others. But we never read conversations where he deals specifically with some grieving person. There are no conclusive steps given whereby grief may be attacked.

THE GRIEF OF CHRIST

This absence of such a prescription does not mean that Christ did not understand grief or that

87

he had not experienced it himself. Anyone who has experienced as much grief and sorrow as Christ did has to feel deeply for others in their grief. He certainly had his own share of hurt, misunderstanding, sorrow, and grief. Isaiah prophesied that he would be "a man of sorrows and acquainted with grief" (Isa. 53:3). The writer of Hebrews says that "He learned obedience by the things which He suffered" (Heb. 5:8). On one occasion he stood above Jerusalem and wept over her soul-bent plight to ruin. Like a hen gathering her brood beneath her wing, he called to Jerusalem, but she could see neither the beauty of the life that he offered, nor the danger of the encroaching Roman powers about her throat. He was frustrated, like a hen trying desperately to communicate to her newly-born chicks the beauty of new life in its basic rudiments and the dangers that lurk around every bush. He grieved their course, and they would not respond.

One of the very early grief experiences of Christ must have been the death of his own father, Joseph. We are not told in Scripture that Joseph died, but the fact that the Scripture ceases to refer to him early in Christ's journey, as well as the fact that Jesus himself became known afterward as the Carpenter of Nazareth, infers that Joseph must have died. Seemingly, at what might have been the age of a teenager, Christ assumed the role of breadwinner for the family. The weight of helping his mother, Mary, rear at least four brothers and sisters, along with the absence of a strong father figure to see him into full manhood, must have been a pressing, if not a grieving, affront to his life.

Because Christ had become an accomplished and well-sought-after carpenter, it is likely he had spent many long and joyous hours following in the footsteps of his father in the carpenter's shop. A genuine intimacy and camaraderie between the two surely must have been developed. The learning of a trade appropriately would require such closeness. The eventual loss of his father in death at such a pliable age as his must certainly have grieved him. An instant vacuum must have pulsed through his timbers. The added responsibility of the family did not lessen but rather compounded his sorrow.

Another pressing experience of grief came to Christ when a runner brought him a message from Mary and Martha that their brother, Lazarus, was on the verge of death. Christ had seen many people die, but the imminent death of his friend struck him especially deeply. How much he had shared in the home of Lazarus and his two sisters! They were his new family, and now the thought of such an intimate relationship ending in death had a paralyzing effect upon him. He stayed in the same place three days, knowing, grieving, before he made the journey to Bethany and to that little home and family that he so dearly loved.

How did Christ handle grief and sorrow? What did he do with the hurt? Well, one would think, considering who he was, that he just bit his lower lip and was tough. Had he done so, he would have demonstrated *unreality* not *reality*. Jesus knew that one of the chief principles of life is the facing of it in all its complexity—to feel it deeply and to deal with it responsibly.

Facing life does not mean giving in to it, but rather admitting our natural feelings about it. We do not alleviate the hurt by deceiving ourselves about its reality. We do not escape by denying it, hiding from it, or sleeping it off. In fact, such responses to it only aggravate it and make its force more pronounced.

Christ faced life head on. He experienced it thoroughly; felt it deeply. He allowed the tension to be expressed, the pain to be suffered. There is no greater example of his response than in the facing of his own death. He had fully assured his disciples of his impending death (John 13—17), but its force was not felt so intensely as when that little group had followed him across the Brook Kedron into Gethsemane (John 18; Mark

14; Matt. 26; Luke 22). In Gethsemane, according to Matthew, "He began to be sorrowful and deeply distressed" (Matt. 26:37). Mark has him reacting with impassioned fervor: "My heart is exceedingly sorrowful, even to death" (Mark 14:34). Another version puts it, "My soul is almost grieving unto death." In his agony the perspiration rolled from Christ's brow as "great drops of blood" (Luke 22:44). Blood seeping through the pores of his skin indicates the intensity of his inner pressure, the reality of the pain. For him, denial was not a realistic approach to pain. The fact that he responded to the will of the Father shows his ability to face duress from the posture of strength and not weakness.

HOW THE DISCIPLES FACED GRIEF

Christ's disciples, on the other hand, were frightened of the impending sorrow. They finally realized that they really were about to lose the best friend they ever had. In their own minds their best course was not to think about it, to hide in the shadows of the gnarled olives, to sleep off their great fear and sorrow. The Gethsemane accounts by Matthew and Mark infer that the disciples merely fell asleep due to exhaustion or even because their care for Christ's struggle was not as intense as it should have been. But when we read the account given by Luke, the physician and the greater historian among the writers, we are left with no speculation. Luke wrote that Christ returned to the disciples and "found them sleeping from sorrow [grief]" (Luke 22:45). The self-accusing question of Christ, "Why do you sleep?", is not an effort to raise their guilt, but rather an attempt to make them face their own escape from reality.

This response to grief on their part was a weakness of character, even if its intensity makes their flight understandable. Though Christ could sympathize with their great concern and fear, there was more than a touch of hurt in his voice when he asked them rhetorically, "What, could you not watch with me for one hour?" (Matt. 26:40). Almost instantly, as if he recognizes that their staying awake would not have changed the grueling ordeal for him, he defers to them kindly: "Sleep on now and take your rest, . . . the Son of man is betrayed into the hands of sinners" (Mark 14:41).

PREPARED PERSONS

Christ, in His own person, shows us how to face the grueling realities of life. He was a prepared person before God who embodied what it takes to confront the overwhelming situations of life. Our exhilarating adventure is, likewise, to become that same kind of "prepared person" which will be capable of facing the pressures, demands, and heartbreaks of our own human pilgrimage. We should know early on that grief and pain are unforgiving toward those who are unprepared persons, those who have not the life of Christ within; for it is, indeed, the principles and character of Christ within us that will be able to withstand the inevitable hurt.

When we give thought to Christ's sensitivity to the hurt around him, as well as his own sorrows, we still wonder why there are no distinct prescriptions for the handling of grief. When we reflect, however, upon what it is that God is wanting to make of us, we are almost persuaded to believe that their absence is intentional. We must not depend upon rules, pat answers, or even solutions that someone outside ourselves might supply for us. God is putting down into the cavernous recesses of our beings the *inner resources* with which to experience life. The principles that he asks us to adopt are inner mandates that make us into bulwarks of Christlikeness. His life is being galvanized into us. His presence is being made the sentry over every heartbeat. The power of that Life and Presence will not only produce "life" in us; it will be adequate to face the onslaughts that would destroy that life—even our undesirable journey through grief.

THE HUMAN HEARTCRY

Thus the situation at the graveside of Lazarus reflects the grieving experience of every person. As Christ stands before the grave, Martha remarks remorsefully to him: "Lord, if you had been here, my brother would not have died" (John 11:21). Christ, apparently, was stricken with this pronouncement as the human heartcry. How could they stake so much on his presence? And yet that seemed to be their comfort. Remember that every act that Christ performed was an action of the character of God himself. His resuscitation of Lazarus was God's response to the human heartcry in the midst of grief. Here is a caring presence. In raising Lazarus, Christ gives back a presence to symbolize the depth of condolence in the heart of God. He was saying, as it were, "This is just a taste of what is coming," and then he gave the basis of all consolation, the nearest thing there is to a formula for grief. He said, "I am the resurrection and the life" (John 11:25).

So, I answer my own question: there are no rules to follow, only principles and a Presence. Those principles and that presence, however, embody all that we need for life's circumstances, joyous or grim. We must resolve with ourselves that Christ never told us that he would lay out life's pathway for us, just as it was not laid out for him. He promised us only two things: *life* and a *presence*—"I have come that they may have life, and they may have it more abundantly" (John 10:10), and "I am with you always, even to the end of the age" (Matt. 28:20). He left us the principles that produce his Life and he gave us his real presence in the Resurrection for implementing those principles. It is no tragedy that there are no formulas, no prescriptions for our grief. Christ has given us better.

Life Can Be Exciting—Again!

And ye, beneath life's crushing load,
    Whose forms are bending low,
Who toil along the climbing way
    With painful steps and slow,

Look now! for glad and golden hours
    Come swiftly on the wing:
I rest beside the weary road,
    And hear the angels sing!
                              —Edmund H. Sears

How shall we sing the Lord's song
In a foreign land?
                              —Psalm 137:4

In the first chapter of this book, I made the following statement which is possibly the most crucial remark central to our grieving experience: "The purpose of grief as a journey is to help us recover our capacity for life, to give us time to regain a renewed vision of purpose, meaning, and excitement about life." What strikes me as almost contradictory to this purpose is the overriding lack of hope that seems always present with those who grieve. Any excitement in life, invariably, appears fleeting. Meaning seems no longer convincing. Although there is hope of regaining new life for the bereaved, they cannot be convinced of it; they must discover it for themselves as part of their own journey.

The journey through grief has its stages, some universal to all, but others quite unique to the individual. When God's purpose and direction are allowed to bear upon the course, stages become exclusively our own. God knows more about the potential stages of grief through which we ought to pass than we might envision for ourselves. Though I am not one who subscribes totally to the theory of "prescribed stages" through which the bereaved "must" pass before they become whole again, there is one level through which all must pass if life is to regain its meaning. That level is the spiritual journey of the *recovery of purpose*. Day-by-day, in spite of life's struggles, I rediscover that due to God's purpose in our lives, life can be exciting again.

A WILLINGNESS OF THE HEART

When what we love and cherish is destroyed before our very eyes, we lose our sense of purpose or at least our zest for living. Unless our hearts are willing to respond to God's movement in our lives, we are certain to find our way back a difficult journey, indeed. Without a vision of intent our rejoinder is plainly that of Job's: "My days are past, my purposes are broken off, even the thoughts of my heart. . . . Where then is my hope?" (Job 17:11, 15). But with the purpose of God open to us, we can become survivors of any tragedy.

Israel found this to be true in the midst of more than one tragedy: her apostasy before God; her refusing the "servant" role which God envisioned for her, and finally the utter destruction of Jerusalem and the Temple and her ultimate exile into Babylonian captivity. Before it was over, her grief and hopelessness would seem endless, but the faithfulness of God to his purpose would prove her misgivings unfounded.

Jeremiah the prophet not only prophesied of her great downfall but of her restoration as well. Her beautiful mirth and gladness in Judah would be taken from her; her joys like that between bride and bridegroom would be stripped from her; the beautiful sound of the millstones grinding her daily grain would be quashed; the oil that fueled her lamps would be depleted; and she would "serve" the Babylonian king for seventy years (see Jer. 25:10–11; 27:22). Just as complete as her losses would also be her restoration: "I will set My eyes on them for good, and I will bring them back to this land; I will build them and not pull them down, and I will plant them, and not pluck them up. Then I will give them a heart to know Me, that I am the LORD; and they shall be My people, and I will be their God, for they shall return to Me with their whole heart" (Jer. 24:6-7). What a doleful, yet exhilarating, preview to such an inevitable and ultimate happiness!

The physical plight of Israel was tragic enough, but her moral failure was most tragic of all. Here was a demoralized people, a people who had lost almost all spiritual vitality: "This is a people robbed and plundered; all of them are snared in holes, and they are hidden in prison houses; they are for prey, and no one delivers; for plunder, and no one says, 'Restore!'" (Isa. 42:22). "There is no one to guide her among all the sons she has brought forth; nor is there any who takes her by the hand among all the sons she has brought up" (Isa. 51:18). Both Isaiah and Jeremiah, however, laid the chief fault at the feet of Israel's spiritual shepherds: "They are shepherds who cannot understand; they all look to their own way, every one for his own gain, from his own territory" (Isa. 56:11); "My people have been lost sheep. Their shepherds have led them astray" (Jer. 50:6).

In the grief of Babylon, Israel lost her song. The psalmist remembered the sadness:

> By the rivers of Babylon,
> There we sat down, yea, we wept,
> When we remembered Zion.
> We hung our harps
> Upon the willows in the midst of it.
> For there those who carried us away captive
>   required of us a song,
> And those who plundered us required of us
>   mirth,
> Saying, "Sing us one of the songs of Zion!"
> How shall we sing the LORD's song in a foreign
>   land? (Ps. 137:1–4)

How we need to learn the providence of God in crisis times, not unlike ancient Israel. How amazed we would be at the prospect of our own hope and purpose though flanked by a deceiving grief. Could we learn the deeper truth of *The Prophet* by Kahlil Gibran when he asserts, "There are no graves here. These mountains and plains are a cradle and a stepping-stone."[1]

Look at the stepping-stones over which God took Israel in order to restore her to her purpose.

First, she was chosen as a "servant" of God to demonstrate to the nations around her what

God is like and what royal purposes he holds for mankind (Isa. 43:9–10; 44:21; Deut. 4–11).

Second, when Israel failed this role but regarded herself as the favorite of God instead of his servant, God uses another servant, Nebuchadnezzar, to bring her to the reality of her role under God. She would learn servanthood by being thrust into a serving role.

God was determined to restore Israel to her vitality: "Behold, I will make you into a new threshing sledge with sharp teeth" (Isa. 41:15). He would, in the third place, call upon another servant to restore her to her freedom and return her to her homeland. In a new act of God the bars of Babylon would be broken down (Isa. 43:14, 18–19), and Cyrus the Great of Elam, King of Persia, would be his instrument (Isa. 44:28; 45:1–5, 13). Here is where the providence of God shines forth as another stepping-stone to his purpose. He would call into his service one who did not know him, yet one who would carry out his providence in the life of Israel.

Cyrus the Great, "whom victory met at every step" (Isa. 41:2), had begun at the age of thirty in Anshan of Media in 559 B.C., and spread with his conquering armies through all of Media, Persia, Mesopotamia, Armenia and finally into Asia Minor. In twenty years this king of empires had conquered lands stretching from the Indus River to the Aegean Sea. What seems strange, though not strange at all when we remember the providence of God, is that Cyrus had bypassed Babylon on his trek Westward. Then at the behest of something within him and at a prescribed moment following the seventy years of Jewish Exile, in 538 B.C. he turned and swept through the plains of Chaldea, conquering as he went, until at last he stood before the gates of Babylon. The people of Babylon themselves opened the gates and Cyrus secured the city, all two hundred and twenty-five square miles of it, without a battle.

The famous Decree of Cyrus freed the Jews to return to Jerusalem in Judah with orders to rebuild the Temple and the city walls. They had gone out of Jerusalem 50,000 strong and returned 60,000 strong. Rejoicing began as the long eight hundred-mile journey from Babylon to Jerusalem got underway. Through Isaiah the prophet God announced: "Behold, my servants shall sing for joy of heart, . . . for behold, I create Jerusalem as a rejoicing, and her people a joy" (Isa. 65:14, 18). "And those among them," he says further, "who escape I will send to the nations . . . and they shall declare My glory among the Gentiles" (Isa. 66:19). God restored her to her purpose as "servants" to demonstrate to the unbelieving nations what God is like in His moral character.

With freedom accomplished, still the stepping-stones were not all intact, for God had a fourth servant who would reside in Judah to shepherd and to mature his people. He would come "as a root out of dry ground" (Isa. 53:2), a Messiah, a Redeemer, to restore spiritual vitality to His people (Matt. 2:5-6; Isa. 53).

What do we make of all this history? The four servants? A people defeated, unable to sing the Lord's song in a strange land? At long last we must see that it means hope, providence, and purpose. And we hear the Lord entreating us as he did Israel: "Sing to the LORD a new song" (Isa. 42:10).

Do you recall my reference earlier to a pastorate of mine and to the death of a beloved deacon? At his memorial service I selected as my text this passage: "How shall we sing the Lord's song in a foreign land?" (Ps. 137:4). When we seem defeated and wiped out by that other tyrant, death, with every good purpose thrown instantly into captivity, we want to express that same complaint. Really, how can we sing? Only because the absolute providence and purpose of God keeps hope alive for us even when we cannot perceive it or when we do perceive it but cannot sing and dance before it. The history of

103

Israel's captivity is incidental if we can learn its lesson: under the loving grace and care of God we shall one day come singing and dancing again.

Look at your own situation! Has God cared for you in your condition, made a way for you, carried you, spoken to you? Is he not trying to weld the broken pieces together, again? Is he not attempting to show you a new joy, give you a new spirit, direct your life into a new day, one with meaning and purpose? Perhaps, then, he knows that the reasons for your misery in the loss of a loved one, have a more far-reaching place than meets the eye. If that is true, that is itself an indication of hope. And if, by the willingness of the heart to respond, you open your life to him, he shall yet make you to sing and dance.

THE PRODIGAL GENEROSITY OF GOD

When something very precious has been *taken* from us, we easily lose our sense of life's generosity and even our belief in the generosity of God. Yet, despite the spiritual vacuum and our own unbelief, God's generosity persists. He cares for us and yearns for us even when we cannot feel his presence. He waits for us to return to belief in the integrity of his character which he holds in our behalf. Such is portrayed, not only in the preceding story of the Babylonian captivity, but also in the parable of the prodigal son (Luke 15:11–32).

To find a story greater than the story of the prodigal son to represent the grandeur of God's generosity would tax us, indeed. If we want to see unconditional love, acceptance, and forgiveness in their rarest forms, we certainly view them best from the posture of the prodigal son's return home to a waiting father. And if when we are beaten down by life, even if we are the chief instruments of our own downfall, or if we feel almost lifeless out in some far country where we have been driven or have chosen to walk—we can renew our vision of the good and noble, the hope and meaning of life, if we can see the open arms of God waiting for us.

We have come to know *agape* in the New Testament as the Greek word for God's kind of love, but it is, also, a word in English which means "open," "gaping," or "unbounded." The love of God is just that, if we understand the generosity and acceptance symbolized by the waiting father in this story. We see in it the striking symbol of the yawning, open, gaping, unbounded arms of the living God.

If we want to capture the central idea in the story, we cannot miss comparing the spirit of the younger son to that of the elder son, and the

105

spirit of the father to that of both sons. Obviously, the story has lost-and-found written all over it, but *lost* would not be lost if generosity were not there from which to slip away, and *found* would not be so found if generosity were not there to which to return.

What is just as surprising is the fact that there is not merely one prodigal in this parable, or even two, but three contrasting prodigals in the strictest sense of that word.

Prodigal, in the Latin, literally means "to drive forth," to do or be something with total abandonment. Moreover, it means to be extravagant, to be lavish or profuse; hence giving or yielding lavishly.

In the mode of the younger son who took his inheritance and went to the far country to live it up, *prodigal* means extravagant in the sense of utter wastefulness—the expenditure of money, time, or effort to an addictive, irresponsible level. Here is the prodigality of self-centered waste!

In the posture of the elder son, *prodigal* means extravagant in the sense of the utter drive toward conservatism and loyalty, to the point of arrogance. Upon the return of the profligate younger son, the elder son had serious qualms about receiving him, perhaps with some justification. To paraphrase his angered response, he says to his father, "Look, all these years I have served you, seeing to the fields; I've never disputed your word; and yet when did you ever throw a party for me and my friends? But just as soon as this scalawag of a son decides to come home, after devouring your livelihood with prostitutes, you welcome him with open arms and kill the fatted calf in his honor" (see Luke 15:29–30). Here is the prodigality of self-centered arrogance.

The father's prodigality is different still, as the extravagance of other-centered love in the face of self-centered wastefulness and self-centered arrogance. Look at the picture. The father loved the younger son who was liberal and adventurous, yet pathetically wasteful and immoral; but he also loved the elder son who was conservative and loyal, yet insecure and arrogant. He not only wanted to restore excitement of life and well-being to his younger son despite his deplorable and inept decision for his own life, but he also expressed utter abandonment in his love and generosity to the elder son: "All that I have is yours!" Here is the prodigality of other-centered generosity—the ultimate extravagance in love.

In brief, look again at the contrast from a spiritual viewpoint. Prodigal number one says, "I want mine! I'm capable of being God for myself!" Prodigal number two says, "God, I hate you for being generous toward such a scalawag as my brother!" But Prodigal number three says, "I want everyone to have his corner in the picture. I'm not willing that any should perish but that all should come to repentance. Yes, I want the prodigal in the far country to repent and I want the prodigal at home to repent. And I'll *wait,* and I'll *love,* and I'll *yearn* until every prodigal is home; and the supper is already prepared!"

Note something very sobering about the stories cited in Luke, chapter 15. We dealt with only one of them, the story of the lost boy. There are, in addition, the stories of the lost sheep and the lost coin. The subjects in all three stories were each lost, and each were lost differently, but the end of each story is strikingly the same. The sheep was lost due to *aimlessness;* it just grazed inadvertently away from the fold. The coin was lost due to *carelessness;* it somehow got away from its negligent owner's grasp. The boy was lost due to *self-centeredness;* he felt that he could be master of his own life and destiny. In the cases of all three parables, however, they hold one thing in common: each ends in a jubilee. In the case of the lost sheep, when the shepherd finds it, "he lays it on his shoulders rejoicing" (v. 5) and calls his friends and neighbors and says, "Rejoice with me, for I have found my sheep which was lost!" (v. 6). In the case of the lost coin, when the woman finds it, she too invokes her friends: "Rejoice with me, for I have found the piece which I lost!" (v. 9). And in the case of the lost boy, after he had sinned against love, he comes home to it, and the waiting father instructs his servants: "Bring out the best robe and put it on him, and put a ring on his hand and sandals on his feet. And bring the fatted calf here and kill it, and let us eat and be merry; for this my son was dead and is alive again; he was lost and is found" (vv. 22–24). The next sentence in the Scripture reads: "And they began to be merry" (v. 24).

Though the far country was far, only one foolish step on the part of the Prodigal landed him in it. And not too many more steps plunged him headlong into an unprecedented hopelessness. But once he "came to himself," only one other step brought him back to the arms of generosity.

For those who feel lost or defeated or hopeless, who sense that life or God have lost their generosity—especially for those who grieve the loss of their beloved—surely this story of the Prodigal gives reassurance. We do not sink so deeply into the cellar of hopelessness but what we can find our way back up in God's generous extravagance on our behalf. Such hope opens the door to our own moment of jubilee.

LIFE IN QUEST OF LIFE

Three days following the burial of those in the plane crash, I wrote a letter to our Christian fellowship, a portion of which is presented here:

The past week has been a traumatically devastating experience for all of us. We have been wiped out emotionally by our losses and bruised deeply by our recall of wonderful memories. There really is no way to understand, rationally, the mysteries surrounding such an event as we have experienced. I'm sure we will keep on trying to do so, however, because although we are people of *faith*, we are also people who want desperately to *know*.

One thing of which we may be relatively certain is that under God's grace such trauma will not turn out to be meaningless, especially after God has been able to move us through the pain. Right now, if the truth were known, meaning and purpose and the heart to fight on, all seem hollow amid our numbness. The truth is, we actually are numb because part of our life has been taken from us. At this point the natural reaction is our hesitancy between two options: 1) that

God might deaden our senses a bit more in order to avert further pain, or 2) that He might quickly flood us with more of his life for facing the terrible feelings of emptiness and fear that we are experiencing. We may even be confused as to which option we prefer.

In reality only one sane option is available, and that is to have the life of God increased within us. In the realm of our suffering we need the oil of God's Spirit poured upon the flickering pilot of our lives until it becomes a conflagration of heat and intensity. We need the life of God unleashed upon our own in order that we may be able to face the tragic in life. Is that not precisely what Christ has come to give us? "I have come that they may have life, and that they may have it more abundantly" (John 10:10). That is life with a small *l* in quest of Life with a capital *L*.

At the Cross however, what Christ had come to give seemed to be destroyed for his most intimate followers. The whole mosaic seemed shattered before them. When great loss of a presence overcomes us, the hopelessness of the situation defeats us. That is distinctly the effect upon Christ's followers when Rome put him on the Cross. If Rome could beat him, what chance did they have? If His own life appeared hopeless, what of their own? Can you imagine the dejection, the utter despair, of those who were trusting him, now watching as his irreclaimable life-blood trickled to the ground? Now, He was dead! And now, He was buried!

The next few days are strange and fearful. The strength of a presence is gone. All support is absent. The world turns ashen. Apparently all is lost and our feelings register the existentialist threat that life after all may be absurd. But we question it all the more, because, although we are people of *faith,* we are also people who want desperately to *know.*

I am surprised now to see that this questioning, this rational desire to make sense out of the sudden loss of a presence, is also biblical. We recall the two despondent people on the road to Emmaus conversing among themselves, bringing up history and prophecy from Moses onward, trying desperately to understand the events that had just transpired at Jerusalem. Already they were trying to put the puzzle together. Already they were wanting to know. Already they were missing the one life that had transformed them. The best friend they ever had, for all they knew, was dead and buried. How could they have been so mistaken about him? Could he really be gone?

That very day, a New Presence was loosed in the world. It was new in that it was the real presence that Christ wanted the world to know. This presence transcended the physical and material limitations of life and proved to be universal and eternal. The Resurrection made this truth available to the human race, and more emphatically the appearances of the Risen Christ confirm its existence.

We are indebted to the great English preacher and thinker, W. R. Maltby[2], for his great views on the meaning of Christ for our lives. No idea of his registers more hope than his interpretation of the appearances of Christ as His final attempt to school his disciples in the reality of his resurrection and his presence even when they could not see him, hear him, or touch him. Christ tried to plant his presence in the unseen so that they, as well as we, affirm it without the use of the senses.

When Mary, for instance, finally recognized the risen Lord that first morning of the Resurrection, she fell unrestrainably at his feet. Just to touch and handle that physical presence again was all-consuming. The response of Christ to her seems curt and a bit crusty, until we understand the reasoning behind his words. He responded, "Do not cling to Me, for I have not yet ascended to My Father!" (John 20:17). She would not cling to him long, or even touch him, for he would ascend to the Father, and she must know the reality of his presence without the sense of touch.

Something of the same schooling develops with the two on the road to Emmaus. As they walk and converse about the wretched Roman events that had ended the life of their Lord, a stranger appears alongside them and takes up their conversation as if he had been present all along. When they come to a fork in the road, the stranger makes as though he would depart their company. Instead, they insist that he come to their home and to dinner. As the honored guest, they allow him to bless and break the bread. Something about his previous conversation on the road, and now the manner in which he blesses and breaks the bread, opens their eyes and they "knew him" (Luke 24:31). The Scripture says that immediately "he vanished from their sight" (Luke 24:31).

On still another occasion as his disciples are gathered in the Upper Room, Christ suddenly appears before them. He marks his presence with some familiar word of peace and joy, and then he is gone. The whole transaction is strange, indeed, for the "doors were shut" (John 29:19). How had he entered? How had he vanished from them?

Again, Christ appears on the shore of Galilee in the presence of his disciples who were coming in from a night of fishing. He has breakfast prepared and eats with them and then passes from them.

This incessant breaking in upon their lives and just as quickly breaking away again begins to establish a new consciousness, that of the reality of his presence. They are in his presence, and then they are not. They see him, and then they do not. They hear his voice, and then all is quiet again. They begin to insist that although they do not see him or hear him and cannot actually reach out and touch him, he is evidently somewhere near. He seems to know all about them. He seems to know where to find them. He seems to be aware of their very conversations. Soon they are saying to themselves, "We do not know where he is, but we know he is somewhere nearby."

Graduation day came the day of the Ascension. Christ disappears from their view for the last time. It is not strange that the Scripture points out that a cloud received him out of their sight (Acts 1:9), thus assuring them that even as they watched him go away, the human sense of sight was instantly cut off, but their vision of a "present" Lord was not.

What do we have here in this final biblical illustration? In the face of death we have a presence regained. A new spirit is loosed upon earth. A

115

new and exciting ministry now lay at the feet of his followers. No longer is the chief symbol of the Christian faith the cross on which Christ died. No, we see beyond the cross to a little band of blood-purchased people standing at the mouth of the empty tomb from which our Lord rose. Resurrection is the central fact and the empty tomb its chief symbol, for it depicts a living Lord, a "real presence" that is infinitely more significant than if Christ stood physically before us.

The circumstances and demeanor of those who saw their Lord die could not have appeared more hopeless and dismal. But the day they learned of the new and vital Presence turned loose in the world, a new life of excitement, vision, and purpose flooded in upon them. One from among them later wrote:

> That which was from the beginning, which we have heard, which we have seen with our eyes, which we have looked upon, and our hands have handled, concerning the Word of Life—the life was manifested, and we have seen, and bear witness, and declare to you that eternal life which was with the Father and was manifested to us—that which we have seen and heard we declare to you, that you also may have fellowship with us; and truly our fellowship is with the Father and with His Son Jesus Christ.

And these things we write to you that your joy may be full. (1 John 1:1–4)

Another from among that early band of witnesses, writing to those dispersed due to the persecution of Christians, said with respect to their revelation of Jesus Christ: "whom having not seen you love. Though now you do not see Him, yet believing, you rejoice with joy inexpressible and full of glory" (1 Peter 1:8).

Even in the face of bitter losses of some loving presence, I do not know of any greater source of joy than the Presence of One who is not only somewhere very near to us but who knows of our sorrows and complaints. The Redeemer of Israel, old and new, the prodigal generosity of the waiting Father, and the real Presence of the living Lord is our only haven of hope. In him, life can be exciting, again!

The Courage to Laugh Again

You will weep and lament, but the world will
rejoice; and you will be sorrowful, but your
sorrow will be turned into joy.

—John 16:20

God has made me laugh.

—Genesis 21:6

Laughter is not solely the chuckle or outright
guffaw over humorously incongruent matters of
life as we experience it. That is, it is not solely a
humorous response to a joking situation. Sometimes it is the deeply refined and spontaneous
reaction to a sense of glory and wonder. Real
laughter, in this sense, is the consequence of a
deep and abiding happiness, yet a happiness
based not on events and circumstances but on a
settled disposition of joy.

Can you imagine the glory and wonder, the ju-
bilant outcry among the followers of Christ when
they first heard of his Resurrection. Their laughter must have reverberated along the leathery
foothills of Galilee, as it were, kicking up the dia-

mond light of a new dawn. But just as quickly ask yourself, "Why?" Nothing had changed. Their circumstances were still the same. The plaintive culture around them was no different the day after the Resurrection than before it. The mob was still out for blood of any who named the name of Christ. Caiaphas, the belligerent high priest, had not forgotten their association with Jesus. Rome limped along just as intolerantly as if nothing important had transpired.

What a misjudgment! Something explosive had happened. Grief and sorrow came alive. Dismay and depression fell away. Humiliation and shame melted down under the white heat of a risen Savior's love. The followers of Christ were no longer timid, defeated personalities. They were changed, and they were changed forever. A new joy bolted into their lives from which they would never again be driven. Though circumstances were the same or worse, the disciples were not. Courage enveloped them; excitement challenged them; joy sustained them. Their disposition was settled.

This settled disposition of joy, borne of courage, eventually changed the ancient world. It was said of those who followed the resurrected Lord, though ungrammared and unlearned: "These are they who have come turning the world upside down" (Acts 4:13 and 17:6). Leslie Weatherhead cited the following statements by W. R. Maltby:

> In the sermon on the mount, Jesus promised His disciples three things—that they would be entirely fearless, absurdly happy, and that they would get into trouble. They did get into trouble, and found, to their surprise, that they were not afraid. They were absurdly happy, for they laughed over their own troubles, and only cried over other peoples'.[1]

How different is our present culture! The usual form of laughter is a diversion from the everyday events of life, lightening our emotional load or covering our pain momentarily.

In stark contrast, however, is the great need for a joy that is a centering upon the deeper values of life. Though we are a people of great concentration, in which every moment is pegged for some chosen priority, we need most, not diversion from the ordinary, but a centering upon the great, the creative, the uncharted splendor of God's purpose moving in our lives. You can never convince Saturday-night man of this, however. He thinks that what he needs, what he is entitled to, is to spread himself aimlessly over the weekend, drumming up whatever bit of fake laughter he can muster, fabricating whatever simulated enlivenment he can design for the moment. The trouble with much of this pointless distraction from real life is that it is followed loathingly by the inevitable cock crow of Monday morning. More often than not, such hilarity is a letdown because one does not feel that his life is increased or fulfilled by it. There is no lasting joy to much of it—to very little of it, in fact.

For the bereaved of modern times, the prayer that they find the courage to laugh again does not advocate some flippant outburst to cover pain. No, the buoyancy of a new kind of laughter will change one's temperament toward the hurt and heal the pain from the inside out. We can never anesthetize ourselves to the world around us with all its hurts and disappointments, but we can confront it with the courageous attitude of Christ which may result in a liberating joy that answers our disillusionment. We are referring here to something that is soul-deep.

LAUGHTER OF THE SOUL

Joy is the laughter of the soul. It transcends ordinary laughter by such illimitable measure, that to have such joy is to have a part of the very heart of God. One of the most prominent characteristics about God is his joy and delight. We know this by the manner in which Christ expressed the content of his life. He faced the almost unbearable challenges of life with a refined disposition of cheerfulness. "Be of good cheer," he said, "I have overcome the world" (John 16:33). What did he mean by that? Whatever else he meant, He certainly meant that he had overcome the world's ways and disposition. His world was a culture that was bleak and foreboding. His delight in life gave a different tone to the world around him, to the point, in fact, that He became its conscience instead of its critic.

In the epigraph that heads this chapter, Christ assures us that we will experience grief, even to its audible expressions of weeping and lamenting. Pathetically, the world, with its shallow hilarity, goes on oblivious to the gravity and genuineness of that experience. Christ adds that we will actually be "thrown into sorrow" or "have cause to grieve," but because we, as Christians, look to another world, our sorrow and grief will be turned into joy. It is little wonder that the Christian can laugh with an overcoming joy: even in the midst of anxiety, there is consequence to his laughter.

Christ was not always happy with his circumstances, but he was always joyful. There is a vast difference in the two. Happiness is dependent upon "happenings" and usually favorable and painless ones. Joy, in contrast, is a settled disposition that rides roughshod over even the bitter events in our lives that would ordinarily shake our faith and sanity. One can have a joy that passes understanding and yet be unhappy or even depressed over some circumstance at the moment. A friend going through some difficult times wrote me a letter recently describing his personal and financial predicament. He expressed his depressed and unhappy lot, and still, with all his struggle to keep hearth and household afloat, he ended his letter by admonishing me: "Be joyful"! That comment itself was almost laughable because of its seeming incongruence with his actual situation. Yet, that is the mark of a true Christian: in spite of his human frustration and suffering from time to time, a divine joy supports him from beneath. Man is born with a whimper but once he is introduced to a joy that dispels inordinate fear, he finds the basis of a peace that is not of this world.

THE VALUE OF JOY AND LAUGHTER

In spite of depression or even pain, joy can persist, and laughter can help it to persist. Laughter heals a lot of wounds and makes our sorrowful plot in life more bearable. On one occasion an automobile parked outside a school for deaf children caught my attention. This car, of course, was not just any ordinary car. On its doors were painted multicolored balloons and an inscription which read: "Professional Clown." Here, in this school, were children deprived of one human function that if not dealt with appropriately could leave a child defeated or frustrated. The joy and laughter that a clown might bring could easily make the difference in the way these children respond to life. Some wise teacher or school principal was grandly sensitive to the emotional needs of those wonderful little children.

The laughter produced in this instance is more than surface, for it is dealing with potential affirmation or illness. Children such as these who are handicapped insofar as their hearing is concerned, can internalize their limitation to the point of becoming constricted, even morbid in life. Or, given a sense of their value and potential by affirming individuals such as the clown and caring teachers, they can shake all forms of personality constriction and learn to express, their inwardness in a wholesome and life-affirming way.

Children, or anyone for that matter, who find a reason for their being and who express their full potential (even in the face of physical limitation) experience deeper joy. Laughter, then, is not only an expression but also a release, of their inner strengths. The noted American psychiatrist, Rollo May, makes this point even more emphatically when he writes:

> Joy is the affect which comes when we use our powers. Joy, rather than happiness, is the goal of life, for joy is the emotion which accompanies our fulfilling our natures as human beings. It is based on the experience of one's identity as a being of worth and dignity, who is able to affirm his being, if need be, against all other beings and the whole inorganic world.[2]

May quotes William Blake as saying that "Energy is Eternal Delight." This can be proven in no greater setting than among those who are experiencing deep grief. Grief so debilitates a person as to leave him emotionally and physically devastated. Grief and sorrow take their toll on all the vegetative signs: appetite is lost; adequate sleep habits are interrupted; sexual drives are diminished; thought processes are disorganized. In a word, a person's energy forces are severely constricted to the point that he does not feel like "doing" anything. This is what C. S. Lewis described as "the laziness of grief." But let that same person begin to experience a little laughter and joy as he works through his grief, and energy of all sorts begins to return. A vitality of thought emerges; invigorating attitudes ensue; sleep becomes more regulated and normal; appetite returns with more constancy; the body itself begins to regain its homeostatic condition.

Norman Cousins, in his book *Anatomy of an Illness,* submitted substantial evidence that the ancient theory of laughter as a good medicine was actually true. Due to the endorphins released from the brain by laughter, Cousins discovered the salutary effect of laughter upon body chemistry and the system's ability to fight inflammation as well as to relieve pain. During his bout with cancer, Cousins reported that "ten minutes of genuine belly laughter had an anesthetic effect" and would give him "at least two hours of pain-free sleep." He went on to report that there was only "one negative side-effect of the laughter from the standpoint of the hospital—he found himself disturbing other patients.[3] One must simply read Cousin's book for himself to discover the amazing healing effects of laughter.

As a result of published experimentations such as that of Norman Cousins', doctors and other health officials are discovering the medicinal rewards of laughter. Research on the usage of entertainment centers in clinics and mental hospitals is becoming an important feature in many health engineering schools. So long as such efforts are kept in perspective, the practice will remain useful and not become merely overridden by diversion.

LAUGHTER, AN OPEN BOOK

The ability to laugh, though flanked by great loss or grief, indicates at least two things: that some laughter comes out of pain and that one knows, by his laughter, that he is not clinically depressed. Though laughter can become both the expression of pain and the expression of pain resolved, we need not go so far as some authorities who are now purporting that all laughter roots in pain. That would be the same as saying that whatever is not laughter is pain, which is not true. So long as it does not become an escape from reality, laughter may be one means of handling pain.

More than a ventilation, however, laughter can serve as a revelation of the true state of affairs going on within us. In this light, laughter becomes an open book to those who are sensitive enough to read deeply.

In my counseling service I listened astutely to

the laughter of my clients, for it gave me clues to their inner condition. Sensitivity to the demeanor of their laughter drew many distinctions. One counselee was so severely handicapped emotionally that the very best of her attempts to laugh were greatly strained. Another counselee, in contrast, though she was quite as emotionally handicapped as the first, found everything an occasion for laughter. Yet the laughter seemed contrived as a cover-up for her misery, or an indication that she was not as ill as presumed. Similarly, a gentleman once sat in my office laughing uncontrollably for the first five minutes of the session. Further into the session, however, he burst into tears in a deluge of anger and depression over a recent divorce. His depression was so severe, in fact, that he had to be placed on medication as an interim measure. Another counselee was quite ill emotionally and severely troubled by hallucinations. She was so defeated that she could not laugh. The absence of laughter in this case also served as a clue to her inner condition. By not laughing, she was being true, at least for the moment, to her perceptive feelings. There came a day, however, when she worked through her anxieties and her hallucinations left her. Her buoyancy and spontaneity of joy returned and with them a natural and realistic laughter.

Just as revealing is the fact that sometimes we who are not severely ill, nonetheless, wear our feelings on our sleeves by the manner in which we laugh. Whatever type it is, whether the expected polite laughter or the spontaneous guffaw, we indicate, to a large extent, what is going on in our lives. A personal experience may be helpful to describe what is meant here. My wife and I were visiting a Mexican family who are friends of ours. I spent most of the time with the husband while Eve spent most of the time with the wife but in close proximity to each other. When we left, Eve told me something that Yadi had said about me. In her broken English, she had remarked to Eve: "He is happy fellow. All time he laugh." At that time I was joyful most of the time and usually found everything a condition for laughter.

There came a time, however, when I allowed my work, along with outside pressures, to browbeat me. Frustration began to defeat me, to the extent that one day a thirteen-year-old neighbor remarked to her mother: "What has happened to Robert? He doesn't laugh anymore. He doesn't seem happy." Needless to say, she had not only sensitively sized up my condition but had dropped a sobering bomb on my pride, for who wants to be a persistent dullard.

It was at this juncture in my life, in the wake of

that remark, that I began to study my responses and reactions in life. So my circumstances were not the best! So what? Should my feelings be endlessly determined by my own circumstances or even by conditions around me? At this point I learned the difference between happiness and joy as I recalled what my beloved college teacher, Nat Tracy, taught us. "Joy," he said, "is a delight in life that runs deeper than pain or pleasure." That recollection along with my own inward search began to cure me, and I began to take on a little more of what Blake describes as "Eternal Delight."

Once we determine that we are going to be people of joy, we begin to move into life with that attitude or disposition settled. We may not have reasons to be happy all the time, but an undercurrent of joy can persist such that it changes us. Then, and only then, do we take measures to change our circumstances; and if we cannot, at least we accept them without their stifling our disposition. Christ said quite bluntly: "Your joy no one will take from you" (John 16:22).

THE PARADOX OF JOY AND SUFFERING

If joy has this enduring effect upon us, then it must mean that suffering and joy can exist side by side. They need not cancel out one another. The apostle Paul once wrote to his friends in Corinth that there were times when his detractors regarded him as "sorrowful, yet always rejoicing"(2 Cor. 6:10). The biblical proverb says, "Even in laughter the heart may sorrow, And the end of mirth may be grief" (Prov. 14:13). Leslie D. Weatherhead, the late minister of City Temple of London, put it succinctly: "For when all has been said about joy, its opposite is not sorrow. Sorrow and joy can be held in the mind together at the same time."[4] Possibly the only beatitude of laughter found anywhere is that one found in the Scripture: "Blessed are you who weep now, for you shall laugh" (Luke 6:21).

In *The Prophet*, Kahlil Gibran said, "Your joy is your sorrow unmasked."[5] Is he not saying that sometimes when we pull the mask down from our sorrow, we find to our amazement our joy lurking behind it? Is our joy indeed our sorrow disguised? Have you ever told a bittersweet story, perhaps of a relationship that has come and gone, a mixture of storm and rainbowed sky, and began to laugh over its amusement until that laughter dredged up the sorrow too, and turned to low sobs and warm tears? And in the course of that solemn recollection, did you not know the source of those tears to be also the source of your joy? Is that not precisely what Gibran meant in the completion of his thought—"And the selfsame well from which your laughter rises was oftentimes filled with your tears."[6] Maybe it is true after all that every cloud has a silver lining.

Could we learn this valid paradox of our laughter and grief without being overly affective or unnatural? When our joy comes into conflict with out sorrow, we are not asking people to be incongruent with reality. Obviously, someone who has just lost a loved one cannot find much reason for laughter. To muster laughter in this instance would be a denial of the pain. To experience that pain as pain is the first natural inclination of the body and the psyche to heal themselves. Only as we recognize this do we also begin to view pain as a gift.

I liked very much what Bett Weedon, a friend of mine, said recently at a Christian retreat in the wake of some of her own losses: "Wouldn't it be tragic if we couldn't hurt!" More illuminating than her words was the expression on her face as she spoke them, for she was smiling through her tears. She was linked up with an "Eternal Delight" that spoke louder than her sorrow. Elton Trueblood wrote in his book, *The Humor of Christ,* that "the well-known humor of the Christian is not a way of denying the tears, but rather a way of affirming something which is deeper than tears."[7] Paul remarked that among the Christians at Macedonia, though they were "in a great trial of affliction" it was "the abundance of joy and their deep poverty" that caused them to give themselves with such rich liberality (2 Cor. 8:2). What a combination: affliction, poverty—yet richness filtering triumphantly from their lives because of joy.

Perhaps the paradox of laughter and suffering existing together is itself a healing mechanism. Without the element of joy, where meaning exists, we would be blown apart in the face of certain grief. Periodic joy rising to the surface, or even the divergence of plain laughter, can be a safety valve against total collapse. C. S. Lewis felt that his jotting of notes (which later became the book, *A Grief Observed*) served as just such a safety valve. But I know that it must be different for others as most persons do not so measurably take stock of their feelings.

Each bereaved person must find his or her own safety valve: For some the safety valve may be the necessity of caring for their small children and helping them through the loss of a mother or father. That in itself is a force or drive that helps one to maintain sanity and reality. For another, the diversion into studies in preparation for a new life and ministry that seems meaningful calls one out of self long enough to release the inner pressure. For still another, the writing of letters and the extending of a ministry or dream already begun by the deceased is the cherished safety valve. Another links up with a valuable, supportive, social cause and finds the centering a means of increasing life for the moment. Getting away into peaceful moments of retreat is another option. The fostering of life in new forms helps one immensely to face the uncertainty of the daily confrontation with grief.

When one adopts the courage to laugh again, he finds a safety valve that releases the undesirable inner pressures. Oh, sure, the laughter will be covered over again by grief's slow anger and the repeated return of sorrow until better days; but the better days may be precipitated by the mysterious healing powers of laughter. C. S. Lewis relates how very difficult such a "program" of intent was for him in thinking of his deceased wife. He wrote: "I will turn to her as often as possible in gladness. I will even salute her with a laugh. The less I mourn her the nearer I seem to her." And yet the difficulty of his doing so met with seeming impossibility, as "all of the hells of young grief . . . opened again."[8] In the final analysis, however, it may be the courage to laugh that eventually makes the impossible possible.

LAUGHTER AS BELIEF

The courage to laugh ultimately rests with our belief in the faithfulness of God. During our grief we will not likely laugh for the right reasons, unless we feel assured that God has a stake in our lives and will come through for us. So then, it becomes our belief behind our laughter that makes the laughter a healing force. God Himself has engendered our laughter, and he becomes the divine enabler of our joy.

Do you recall the episode in Old Testament history (Gen. 18:13–15; 21:1–7) of Sarah's bearing Isaac in her old age? When the messengers of the Lord came to Abraham and told him that Sarah would bear a child, she overheard them from inside the tent. At first she laughed jokingly, almost in derision, of the disparity to bear a child at such an age. If God can be shocked, he was certainly shocked at Sarah's faithless reaction. He put the incontestable question to Abraham: "Why did Sarah laugh? . . . Is anything too hard for the LORD" (Gen. 18:13–14). When the child was born, "at the set time of which God had spoken" (Gen. 21:2), Sarah laughed for a different reason— from the joy of bearing Abraham a son from conditions of seeming impossibility. Her response at this point was no longer one of derision but one of elation and belief: "God had made me laugh, so that all who hear will laugh with me" (Gen. 21:6). It is no surprise that they named the child *Isaac* which means "Laughter"!

When we laugh with God through the very life that He incites within us, not only are we healed of our disbelief, but we are reminded of the very wellspring of our joy, almighty God Himself, as Paul called him—"the blessed (happy) and only Potentate, the King of kings, and Lord of lords" (1 Tim. 6:15).

When we are able to laugh because of the expanded life of God within, we also engender that laughter in the world. We need not be surprised that the soul-deep laughter of Sarah in turn begat soul-deep laughter. "He who has laughter," wrote Frederick Speakman, "God's brand, not the mocking kind that flays, but the little bells that heal, such a man will draw laughter to him. But he who has none will lose even the faint echoes of it."[9]

A FINAL INQUIRY

In conclusion, to those who journey through grief, may I entertain one final inquiry? What do you like and respond to best among your friends? Of course, you love their warmth and kindness; you like their availability and large-heartedness; you even understand and respond to their sadness and frustration; but best of all, you like them when they are laughing with you, for not only does that feature seem to embody all the others, but it elicits the quality and depth of your own joy.

What is it precisely that you remember best about that beloved person in your life whom you lost in death? Is it not the laughter you remember, when you recall the way you were?

Out of such suffering love recalled, please take courage to laugh again, and so elicit from those around you a strength that will cancel their defeat and resurrect your own illimitable joy. Because God holds the blueprint of your living and your dying, he holds the destiny of your sorrow, too, and gives to you the gift of laughter once more.

EPILOGUE
Sin's Biggest Failure—The Death of a Christian

———○———

"Death is swallowed up in victory. . . .
O Death, where is your sting?
O Hades, where is your victory."
—1 Corinthians 15:54, 55

"I have set before you life and death, blessing
and cursing; therefore choose life . . . ."
—Deuteronomy 30:19

All that *Sin* can possibly heap upon us is currently at work attempting its prize victory—that victory being our moral and spiritual defeat. At times its severity is so great that it appears as though it might actually succeed. If Sin can demoralize us, we lose! If it can destroy the preciousness of life by showing us how stern and determined death can be, then it wins and we end in despair! If Sin can ultimately separate us from the heart of God, then all is lost.

Grief would be comfortless if Sin were allowed

to carry out its intent. If it can win the battle in life, it certainly will win the battle in death. In the life of the Christian, however, Sin will be defeated on both frontiers. We may take comfort, then, in knowing that grief is a trial journey for testing the credibility of a faith that cannot be shaken. Those who have been taken from us in death are tasting sweet victory; those of us who linger behind are experiencing a sting that cannot ultimately destroy.

This overcoming solace is the good news of salvation which Christ has put within our reach. We no longer serve the indefatigable warfare of Sin, rather the winning glory of God. The prophet Isaiah envisioned not only our redemption but our comfort through the promised Redeemer:

The Spirit of the Lord GOD is upon me,
. . . .

To comfort all who mourn,
To console those who mourn in Zion,
To give them beauty for ashes,
The oil of joy for mourning,
The garment of praise for the spirit of heaviness;
That they may be called trees of righteousness,
The planting of the LORD, that He may be
    glorified.

(Isa. 61:1a, 2c, 3)

139

God set before us life, but Sin, which entered the human race through Adam, purports to take it from us. However, because God remains in the picture, Sin ultimately loses, and its greatest defeat is death itself, for death is its last stronghold.

From its very entrance into the world, Sin changed the prime destiny of man. Prior to its beginning in man there was no spiritual or physical death because God had created a perfectly ordered world of harmony based on his own life. Anthropology itself has not proven the animal origin of man, nor has it clarified for us the reason for death in man, either from a scientific or a philosophical analysis. Paul Tournier remarks: "Since nothing in nature explains death, there is nothing to oppose the idea that this man did not die so long as there was nothing that disturbed the perfect harmony of this perfect world."[1]

As the Bible states, however, *something* did enter to disturb this pristine harmony—a sinister root evil called "Sin," which even itself eludes definition except to say that it is mysteriously engrained against God and causes the disharmony that exists in the moral nature of man and in the physical nature of the universe itself (see Romans 8). Oh, don't blame sin on the Devil, whatever you do. The Devil is the product of sin. He may now be its harbinger in our conscience, our tempter, our liaison to evil, but he is not the rationale for the evil we do nor for the disaster we suffer. They are all "symptoms" of the deeper "cause." According to the Bible, the "symptoms" of Sin are the sins, iniquities, derelictions, brokenness, and fragmentation of human life on all levels. The ultimate consequence is that death reigns—both spiritual and physical (1 Cor. 15:21). Paul put it quite succinctly, along with its remedy: "For the wages of sin is death, but the gift of God is eternal life in Christ Jesus our Lord" (Rom. 6:23).

From the very beginning God offered man a choice: life or death; blessing or curse (Deut. 30:19). Man's plight and destiny depended clearly upon the choice he made. If he chose to be the sole architect of his destiny, cutting God out of the drama altogether, he would destroy himself. Stark humanism as a way of life proves this point on a daily basis, so that "death" and "curse" seem to reign in its wake. If man, on the other hand, chose to be a partial architect in partnership with his Maker, as God intended it, then he ultimately was choosing "life" and "blessing".

Accordingly, the central point to be made in this epilogue is twofold: 1) Apart from God's redemptive acts in history and ultimately in Jesus Christ, Sin will destroy the moral life of man and bring his rightful destiny to despair; and 2) For the Christian, death itself will be Sin's darkest day and its clearest symbol of its own absolute defeat.

The only way in which we can adequately describe Sin is by its destructive impact upon our lives. It is like the devastation of a tornado. Ten different persons, in trying to describe the force of the storm, may depict its essence in ten different ways; but the destruction in the wake of the storm is never misleading. One knows a tornado best by the destruction it leaves behind. One also knows Sin best by the damaged lives it leaves by the wayside. Apart from the redemptive acts of God the human race is destined to failure and final destruction. Sin will see to that!

In the life of a Christian, however, Sin ultimately displays its greatest defeat—*it cannot complete its own intent*. It cannot carry out its own purpose, which is to so demoralize the Christian as to drive him from the heart of God. Therefore, we need to view the process of Sin that, but for the spiritual life of Christ, begins in deception and ends in death, both physical and spiritual. In following this process there will be ample evidence as to why the death of a Christian is Sin's ultimate defeat.

The two chief frontiers of Sin are deception of one's true relationship to God and distortion of one's true nature as man. In *A Place to Belong*,[2] I delineated in some detail these two frontiers. For the sake of showing Sin's inability to carry out its intent, allow me to outline the process somewhat differently here.

First, Sin dares to convince us that we are the sole proprietors of our own lives. Sin attempts to deceive us into believing that we are not only the custodians of our own dignity but also the harbingers of our own destiny. This puts man at the center and God on the periphery, if he is even allowed a legitimate place at all. In this manner Sin seeks to destroy the whole conception of man as having been created in the "image of God." Were it not for Jesus Christ who restores this image in the believer, Sin would win the war in this first skirmish. Man would go on trying to be his own God, the poor, inadequate sovereign that he has proven himself to be, many times over.

Secondly, Sin dares to separate us from the heart of God. Sin succeeds again and again here because our love for God does not run deeper than the devotion to our own lives. This is why we are always drifting to one side. And we drift far more easily when confronted by the pressures and problems of life.

The healing of this apostasy, this drifting to one side, is precisely the goal of Christ's commitment to our lives. He pledges to the Father, upon the integrity of his own character, that he will take this Christian heart of ours, which is distorted and fragmented, which is beggarly and false, and he will pump all the resources of his grace into that heart, until one day he will present to God a being of beauty and symmetry that can no longer be divided by the onslaughts of Sin. For Christ's victory on the Cross against Sin and his triumph over death in the Resurrection is an eternal accomplishment: no longer can Sin drive a wedge between his heart and the Father's heart. Christ, in turn, pledges to all who trust him the same eternal accomplishment.

Third, Sin dares to deteriorate human character, to demoralize and weaken its integrity. The greatest war ever waged was the struggle between Christ and Sin on the Cross. How easily Christ could have renounced his commitment as Saviour of the world. How easily he could have relinquished the Servant-heart and allowed mankind to fend for itself. How easily he might have denied the integrity of His moral character. But this is precisely what he could not do. He chose to complete the divine mosaic of redemption by remaining on the Cross. He chose to complete the integrity of his being before God. Instead of the joy that lay before him, he endured the

Cross, despising its shame, and was able at last to "recommend" himself to the Father—"Into your hands I commend My spirit" (Luke 23:46). Sin was unable to deteriorate his character. It could not break down his integrity before God.

Sin wages the same battle against the character of man and in so doing attacks God who created it. Delusion and distortion are Sin's greatest devices of spiritual warfare. If it can convince man that he is the arbiter of his own will and the source of his own life, then he no longer needs to answer for his moral character. Sin then deteriorates the integrity of conscience and deludes man into thinking that he is an adequate conservator of his own character.

Very little time is required to see how dismally man has been able to maintain his own dignity, how pathetically he has been able to conserve a respectable character. Left to himself he destroys all moral and ethical thinking and becomes a contradictory being. Meant to bear an intelligent, moral conscience, he stumbles blindly without moral direction. Meant to be a willing desirous being, he is driven into wrong choices and decisions. Meant to be imaginative and creative, he becomes uninventive and destructive. Meant to be basically other-centered, he becomes totally self-centered, uncaring, and insensitive to life going on around him. Meant to

145

bear rational and moral affection for the giving and receiving of love, he becomes indifferent, if not totally hostile. Meant to be whole and mature, he becomes inwardly divided and fragmented. Meant to be a related being, he becomes utterly alone. Sin deludes him, distorts his spiritual vision and ultimately deteriorates his character.

The picture changes radically when Christ takes the helm. He pledges on the basis of his own character to the Father that he will restore this distorted, deteriorated being to his own image. The finished product will have real character—one who can love without self-centeredness, one who can suffer without bitterness, one who can forgive without conditions, one who can give hope in a hopeless age, one who can bear strength in a day of crisis. In a word, Christ will bring the Christian to the place where he can out-live, out-give, out-love, out-laugh, out-cry, and out-last any other being around him. If, in fact, Christ does this in man, Sin can no longer complete its own intent.

Thus, the intent of Sin has been threefold: to convince man that he is his own sovereign; to drive a wedge between his heart and the heart of God; and to deteriorate his moral character. If Christ wins this battle for *life*, then Sin has only one recourse—to win the battle in *death*. This, Sin dares to do on two frontiers.

On the first frontier, Sin seeks to bring a sense of extinction in death. How many philosophies, and even religions, in the world purport that death ends all. Death is not viewed as being part of life or even the transition point into a higher life. It is viewed merely as the final human event tacked onto the end of life. The motto of the Epicureans was "Let us eat and drink for tomorrow we die" (1 Cor. 15:32).

These convinced that death is certain extinction deny the continuity of personality through the resurrection of the dead. From a purportedly scientific viewpoint they deny even the *possibility* of resurrection and therefore make the same spurious pronouncement upon the Resurrection of Jesus Christ, as well.

The Resurrection of Jesus Christ, however, abides the attack by virtue of ample historical evidence to the contrary. Not merely in religious and biblical writings is the Resurrection of Christ convincing, but in secular writings as well—especially in letters of the Roman procurators to the Roman emperor. Though historians cannot explain the Resurrection, they indeed have reported it as an actual fact.

Historical evidence for the Resurrection is

one thing, but moral evidence of the Resurrection is even greater. The real proof of the resurrected life of Jesus Christ is the "resurrected life" of every true Christian. And that "resurrected life" in all its spiritual essence occurs now, not merely awaiting its final expression in bodily resurrection after death. This is why Paul could write to the Roman Christians that they must once for all "present themselves to God as being alive from the dead" (Rom. 6:13). Morally and spiritually they had already escaped the reign of death by joining in the "reign of life" in the resurrected Christ (Rom. 5:17). The sweeping change of their character into one like Christ's moral character verifies that they were already sharing in his resurrection.

Just a few years later, in A.D. 62, Paul would share with the Christians at Philippi his one solicitous desire: "that I may know Him and the *power of His resurrection* and the fellowship of His sufferings, being *conformed* to His death, if, by any means, I may attain to *the resurrection from the dead*" (Phil. 3:10–11, Italics added). He meant, of course, that he was progressively being restored from spiritual death that reigns apart from Christ and His resurrected life. This is indicative of why he had previously called the Roman Christians to live, as Christ now lived, in unbroken relation to God (Rom. 6:10–11) and as "being alive from the dead" (Rom. 6:13). The fuller context is absolutely exhilarating:

> For if we have been united together in the likeness of His death, certainly we also shall be in the likeness of His resurrection, knowing this, that our old man was crucified with Him, that the body of sin might be done away with, that we should no longer be slaves of sin. For he who has died has been freed from sin. Now if we died with Christ, we believe that we shall also live with Him, knowing that Christ, having been raised from the dead, dies no more. Death no longer has dominion over Him. For the death that He died, He died to sin once for all; but the life that He lives, He lives to God. Likewise you also, reckon yourselves to be dead indeed to sin, but alive to God in Christ Jesus our Lord. (Rom. 6:5–11)

During the same period of time, about A.D. 57, Paul wrote to the Christians at Corinth relating that it was by the grace of God that he had become what he now was in relation to the resurrected Christ. He regarded himself, though, as one "born out of time," that is out of proximity to the days in which Christ walked the earth in the flesh. He delineates Christ's resurrection appearances in which he was first seen by Cephas and then by the Twelve, then by over five hundred believers, most of whom were still living contemporaries of his some twenty-five years later. Christ was also seen by James and then by all the apostles. Finally, Paul claims that Christ was seen by him, too, but out of proximity to the others (1 Cor. 15). Out of his experience with the Living Christ on the Damascus road (Acts 9), Paul gained the message of the good news and later refined it under the tutelage of the Holy Spirit for three years in the Arabian Desert. He later inquired in Jerusalem of eye witnesses to the death and resurrection of Christ as to the content of his message and found that his own post-dated experience matched theirs. Here were contemporaries who experienced the same Christ and the same message only twenty-five years apart in time. What greater evidence can be offered for the historical reality of the Resurrection? That evidence would even stand up in a court of law, Roman or otherwise.

We must admit, as Paul does, that if Christ was not resurrected, then our faith is a mere delusion and we remain under the penalty of Sin (1 Cor. 15:17). If Christ has not been raised, then Sin has indeed won the battle for extinction, for "then also those who have fallen asleep in Christ have perished" (1 Cor. 15:18). Then he adds: "But now Christ is risen from the dead, and has become the firstfruits of those who have fallen asleep. For since by man came death, by Man also came the resurrection of the dead. For as in Adam all men die, even so, in Christ all shall be made alive" (1 Cor. 15:20-22).

But someone is sure to ask, "'How are the dead raised up? And with what body do they come?'" (15:35). Paul uses a kernel of wheat giving up its life in one form (the seed) to take up life in another form (the plant). He draws the analogy of differing bodies of flesh (man, cattle, birds, fish) and the heavenly and earthly bodies (the sun, moon and stars as compared to earth). Then he likens this with the resurrection of the dead: "The body is sown in corruption, it is raised in incorruption. It is sown in dishonor, it is raised in glory. It is sown in weakness, it is raised in power. It is sown a natural body, it is raised a spiritual body" (1 Cor. 15:42-44). Then, in this epic on the resurrection Paul gives us that great passage of brilliant rhetoric:

> Now this I say, breathren, that flesh and blood cannot inherit the kingdom of God; nor does corruption inherit incorruption. Behold, I tell you a mystery: We shall not all sleep, but *we shall all be changed*—in a moment, in the twinkling of an eye, at the last trumpet. For the trumpet will sound, and *the dead will be raised*

incorruptible, and we shall be changed. For this corruptible must put on incorruption, and this mortal must put on immortality. So whem this corruptible has put on incorruption, and this mortal has put on immortality, then shall be brought to pass the saying that is written: "Death is swallowed up in victory." "O Death, where is your sting? O Hades, where is your victory?" The sting of death is *sin,* and the strength of sin is the law. But thanks be to God, who gives us the victory through our Lord Jesus Christ. (1 Cor. 15:50–57, italics added. See also Isa. 25:8 and Hos. 13:14)

Now, at length, we can reaffirm our point—Sin fails to bring extinction in death. Sin would be better off if it *could* keep Christians alive. At least then it would have a fighting chance.

Sin has its final chance of success in its second frontier to win the battle in death. It seeks *to demoralize God's people (the survivors) in the face of those who have died.* Here is Sin's rationale personified:

1) If I (Sin) can raise *anger at God* in those who lose loved ones, that will be my quickest route to victory. If I can raise doubt as to the true love and care of God, then I may convince the Christian of the insanity of trusting in a Being who, in fact, allows tragedy and suffering to happen.

2) If I can encourage the *enthronement of grief* in the survivors, I will eventually weaken their defenses until they begin to curse life, everyone around them, and every spiritual principle they ever learned. I'll drag them through grief for years on end, never giving them a reprieve from their suffering and loss, until even God himself will be thought to be sick of them, as well. When this happens, I win the victory.

3) If I can convince them of the *vacuousness of life* in the face of their losses, I will extract every ounce of purpose and motivation from their lives. This will kill their creativity, their contribution and ultimately their witness for God. Then, see how quickly I'll take control!

4) If I can *enthrone loneliness* by the stifling of joy, I will create such misery as will break down every godly smile, every sanctioned hope, and every will to win. There will be no place else to turn.

5) Chief of all, if I can *demoralize them into forgetting the rudiments of their Christian heritage,* they will soon push God aside as a lost cause. I'll get them to renounce the "essence of the good news" which they once "accepted," upon which they always "stood," and through which they were "to be saved." I will thereby stifle their commitment to reflecting the likeness of the Man from heaven, because they no longer

153

sense his presence or feel his power to handle their defeat.

The reason, however, that Sin cannot accomplish these choice objectives is because Jesus Christ helps us become the kind of people that Sin and Death cannot destroy. "For the law of the Spirit of life in Christ Jesus has made me free from the law of sin and death" (Rom. 8:2). Oh, we will stumble; we will wince; we will at times cry out against the threat of despair. Sure, we will entertain feelings about quitting; we will become stowaways for a time, hiding from God. We will find ourselves pummelled and broken, at times bleeding, sometimes giving up more spiritual ground than we claim, moving into life at a mere sluggish pace—sluggish about God, ourselves, our world. We will experience these things and more, but we will experience them falling forward, for "we are not of those who draw back to perdition but of those who believe to the saving of the soul" (Heb. 10:39). Sure, we *want* the easy way out, but *we won't take it!* We desire the broad way, but we will move upon the narrow path that leads to Life at the last possible instant. God, in Christ, has interposed with a promise and a pledge so that "we might have strong consolation, who have fled for refuge to take hold of the hope set before us. This hope we have as an anchor of the soul, both sure and steadfast, and which enters the Presence behind the veil, where the forerunner entered for us . . ." (Heb. 6:18-20).

The Christian battles, then, with an imperishable quality in life, which Sin cannot defeat. That quality is indefatigable in the face of suffering and death. Here are just a few of its characteristics:

1) *Purity in the face of impurity.* God's people are all-soul, all-heart, unalloyed, unvarnished. This is why they will see God and understand Him.

2) *A guiding conscience in a lost and failing world.* This is the chief reason why God's people are called sons of the Light—they are to be the light of the world, healing moral blindness, lighting moral darkness, being a source of warmth for moral coldness.

3) *A renewing, preserving quality in the midst of a dying, putrifying world.* God's people are the salt of the earth working their healing, penetrating force into the wounds of time.

4) *Vitality in a sloven generation.* God's people are full of life and force, standards of strength and enthusiasm, because they are "in God" *en theos* (in God) = *enthu*siasm.

5) *Unselfishness in a self-centered world.* The Christian pushes other people into first place and assumes an unheralded back seat.

6) *A loving response to a people of apathy and*

155

scorn. The Christian's negative reactions to life grow weaker; his positive responses grow stronger.

7) *An abundant quality in an age of emptiness.* God's people assume a quality of life that is abundant in the sense of being as full as it can possibly be lived, constantly improving, increasing, abounding in rich satisfaction.

These are only a few of the qualities that are imperishable. With these alone, the Christian never fails to have the inward resources to meet the challenges and problems of life. Therefore, he never fears what might happen. He is never filled with a sense of futility. He is equal to all occasions. He lives above this world, though in the heart of it, possessing powers that are not of this world, but which will heal this world—even its suffering and grief.

So, I conclude where I began—*Sin's biggest failure is the death of a Christian.* In death, the Christian comes to the ultimate battlefield, and the enemy cannot be found.

NOTES

Chapter 1

1. Gladys Hunt, *Close To Home,* Reflections on Living and Dying (Discovery House Publishers, Grand Rapids, MI, 1990), 61. Used by permission.
2. Blaise Pascal, *Pensées,* translated with an Introduction by A. J. Krailsheimer (London, England: Penguin Books, 1966), 43.
3. C. S. Lewis, *A Grief Observed* (First published in London, England by Faber and Faber, Ltd., N. W. Clerk, 1961, the Seabury Press edition, 1963, and Bantam edition, 1976), 9.
4. John Woolman, *The Journal of John Woolman,* The John Greenleaf Whittier Edition Text (Secaucas, NJ: The Citidel Press, 1972), 222.
5. John Claypool, *Tracks of A Fellow Struggler* (Dallas, TX: Word, Incorporated, 1974), 57.
6. W. O. Carver, *The Self-Interpretation of Jesus* (Nashville, TN: Broadman Press), 94.
7. Claypool, *Tracks of A Fellow Struggler,* 103.

Chapter 2

1. Creath Davis, *Lord, If I Ever Needed You It's Now!* (Palm Springs, California: Ronald N. Haynes Publishers, Inc., 1981), 77.
2. Clark E. Moustakas, *Loneliness and Love* (Englewood Cliffs, New Jersey: Prentice-Hall, Inc., 1972), 55. Reprinted by permission of the publisher.

3. Moustakas, 10.
4. Henri J. M. Nouwen, *The Wounded Healer* (Garden City, New York: Doubleday & Company, Inc., 1972; Image Book edition, 1979), 100.

Chapter 3

1. Joshua Loth Liebman, *Peace of Mind* (New York, NY: Simon and Schuster, 1946), 110.
2. Paul Tournier, *Escape From Loneliness* (Philadelphia, PA: The Westminster/John Knox Press, 1962), 26–27.
3. Liebman, *Peace of Mind*, 112.
4. Tournier, *Escape From Loneliness*, 10.
5. Viktor Frankl, *Man's Search For Meaning: An Introduction to Logotherapy* (Boston, MA: Beacon Press, 1959), 59.
6. Frankl, 60.
7. Liebman, *Peace of Mind*, 111.

Chapter 5

1. Kahlil Gibran, *The Prophet*, Reprinted by permission of Alfred A. Knopf, Inc. Copyright 1923 by Kahlil Gibran and renewed 1951 by Administrators C.T.A. of Kahlil Gibran Estate and Mary G. Gibran.
2. W. R. Maltby, *Meaning of the Cross and the Resurrection* (Nashville, TN: Publishing House M.E. Cherck, South [N.D.]).

Chapter 6

1. Leslie Weatherhead, *Jesus and Ourselves* (London, England: The Epworth Press, 1930), 253, quoting W. R. Maltby, *Christ and Human Need*, 196.

2. Rollo May, *Man's Search For Himself* (New York, NY: W. W. Norton & Company, Inc., 1953), 84.

3. Norman Cousins, *Anatomy of An Illness* (New York, NY: W. W. Norton & Company, Inc., 1979), 39–40, 86.

4. Leslie D. Weatherhead, *This is The Victory* (London, England: Hodder and Stoughton, 1940), 197. Used by permission of Edward England Books Literary Agency, East Sussex, England.

5. Gibran, *The Prophet*, 29.

6. Gibran, 29.

7. D. Elton Trueblood, *The Humor of Christ* (New York, NY: Harper and Row, Copyright © 1964 by Elton Trueblood), 32.

8. C. S. Lewis, *A Grief Observed*, 66.

9. Frederick B. Speakman, *The Salty Tang* (Westwood, NJ: Fleming H. Revell Company, 1954), 103.

Epilogue

1. Paul Tournier, *The Whole Person in a Broken World* (New York, NY: Harper and Row Publisher, Copyright © 1964 by John Doberstein), 115.

2. Taken from the book, *A Place To Belong* by Robert A. Williams. Copyright © 1972 by Robert A. Williams. Used by permission of Zondervan Publishing House.

ABOUT THE AUTHOR

———o———

Member of Park Cities Baptist Church in Dallas, Texas, Robert A. Williams holds a Bachelor of Divinity and Master of Theology from Southwestern Baptist Theological Seminary in Fort Worth, Texas, and has specialized clinical training in marriage and family counseling. Williams is the former director of the lay training center for Christian Concern Foundation in Dallas, Texas, and founder of Ministry of Helps to the Underprivileged. Robert lives with his wife, Evelyn, in Dallas.